William Henry Whitmore

The Massachusetts civil List for the colonial and provincial Periods

1630-1774

William Henry Whitmore

The Massachusetts civil List for the colonial and provincial Periods
1630-1774

ISBN/EAN: 9783337153571

Printed in Europe, USA, Canada, Australia, Japan

Cover: Foto ©ninafisch / pixelio.de

More available books at **www.hansebooks.com**

THE

MASSACHUSETTS CIVIL LIST

FOR THE

Colonial and Provincial Periods.

1630-1774.

THE

Massachusetts Civil List

FOR THE

COLONIAL AND PROVINCIAL PERIODS,

1630-1774.

BEING A LIST OF THE NAMES AND DATES OF APPOINTMENT

OF

ALL THE CIVIL OFFICERS

Constituted by Authority of the Charters, or the Local Government.

BY

WILLIAM H. WHITMORE, A.M.

ALBANY:
J. MUNSELL, STATE STREET.
1870.

PREFACE.

In the following pages an attempt has been made to furnish lists of all the civil officers appointed under the authority of the two charters of Massachusetts, from the first settlement of the colony until the overthrow of the Royal government, together with the dates of such appointments. Such a work, if faithfully executed, can hardly fail to be of service, and it has been the object of the compiler to strive for accuracy in every detail given. The names and dates have been taken from the official records, and such as have not been copied by him personally, have been transcribed by Mr. William B. Trask, a gentleman eminently qualified to do the work thoroughly and accurately. The method pursued was to copy all the civil appointments as they stood on the record, after which these facts were classified and arranged by the compiler. It would hardly be possible to escape some errors in so large a collection of names and dates; but it is hoped that the care exercised in the work of collection and classification has reduced the mistakes to an inconsiderable number.

In these lists will be found the names of the comparatively few civil officers appointed under the first charter, as well as of the far greater number rendered necessary by the increase of the province under its second charter. To render the record more nearly complete it has seemed best to include even the lowest grades of commissioned officers, those of justice of the peace and coroner. An examination of the names, however, will convince the reader that these offices were formerly held in higher estimation than they may be to-day, and that they formed the first steps in the political life of many of the most distinguished men. For the genealogist and local historian these lists will possess a peculiar interest.

The explanations given at the commencement of each list render any general description here unnecessary. It may be said, however, of the lists of the judges, that though comparisons were made throughout with the valuable *Judicial History of Massachusetts* by Hon. Emory Washburn, the facts here given have all been taken from the original records, and add materially to his collections. Especially may be mentioned the records of the counties of York, Lincoln and Cumberland, now in the limits of Maine, but in fact during the Provincial period constituting a portion of Massachusetts, of which he took no notice.

As this book is only intended to be an aid to the student, it was deemed unadvisable to attempt notes on the many interesting topics suggested by it. The constitution of the courts, the causes of appointments or dismissals, the extensive changes in political bodies like the council, are all matters suggested by an examination of these lists, but even the briefest discussion of them would require too much space.

One general conclusion alone may be stated. These lists will indicate clearly that prior to the Revolution, the offices, if not the controlling power, were in the hands of a few families, and other investigations will show these families to have been closely allied by marriages. From this state of affairs the Revolution rescued us; the reader will doubtless form his own opinion as to the influence the presence of such an oligarchy had in causing that event.

In conclusion, the compiler has to express his thanks to A. C. Goodell, Jr., Esq, for valuable assistance in relation to dates procured in England, and to the commissioners for the republication of the Province Laws, for an arrangement by which the use of stereotype plates was secured.

W. H. W.

Boston, Oct., 1870.

TABLE OF CONTENTS.

LIST OF CIVIL OFFICERS.

LIST OF CIVIL OFFICERS.

COLONIAL PERIOD, 1629–1686.

The charter granted by Charles I to certain persons, creating them "one body politique and corporate in fact and name, by the name of the Governor and Company of the Mattachusetts Bay in New England," is dated March 4, 1628–9. It provides for yearly elections of a governor, deputy-governor and eighteen assistants, on the last Wednesday in Easter term, in the general court or assembly of the company. The officers named in the charter are:

MATHEW CRADOCK, *Governor*,
THOMAS GOFFE, *Deputy Governor*,

and as assistants

Sir Richard Saltonstall,	Symon Whitcomb,	Thomas Adams,
Isaac Johnson,	Increase Nowell,	Thomas Hutchins,
Samuel Aldersey,	Richard Perry,	John Browne,
John Ven,	Nathaniel Wright,	George Foxcraft,
John Humfrey,	Samuel Vassall,	William Vassall,
John Endecott,	Theophilus Eaton,	William Pinchon.

Before this date (in 1624), a settlement had been commenced at Salem, and both Roger Conant and John Endecott have been graced with the title of governor. Our use of the term will however be limited to those who were the heads at once of the company and of the colony, thus fulfilling the idea conveyed by the charter. Cradock was governor of the company and Endecott of the settlement, but John Winthrop was the first governor of Massachusetts under the first charter, after the consolidation of the duties and powers belonging to that office. The date of the election of charter officers, after the establishment of the settlement here, was the last Wednesday of Easter term in each year. The election at first was by the whole body of freemen assembled together, but this mode proving inconvenient as the number of settlements increased, various alterations were made.

In 1632 (*Mass. Rec.* I, 95), it was voted "that the Governor, Deputy Governor and Assistants should be chosen by the whole court of Governor, Deputy Governor, Assistants *and freemen*, and that the Governor shall always be chosen out of the Assistants," and this rule seems to have lasted for two years. In May, 1634, however, eight towns sent representatives, and the general court then passed two apparently inconsistent votes. It declared (*Mass. Rec.* I, 117), that "none but the General Court hath power to make and establish laws, nor to elect and appoint officers, as Governor, Deputy

Governor, Assistants, Treasurer, Secretary, Captain, Lieutenants, Ensigns, or any of like moment, or to remove such upon misdemeanor, as also to set out the duty and powers of said officers." But it also decreed (*Mass. Rec.* I, 118–9), that it should be lawful for the freemen of each town to depute two or three persons " to deal in their behalf in the public affairs of the Commonwealth," who should " have the full power and voices of all the said freemen, derived to them for the making and establishing of laws, granting of lands, &c., and to deal in all other affairs of the Commonwealth wherein the freemen have to do, *the matter of election of magistrates and other officers only excepted, wherein every freeman is to give his own voice.*"

From this we may conclude that the second statement controlled the first, and that it was necessary to have a mass meeting for the election of officers.

Winthrop (*Hist.* I, 159, old ed.), says of the election in 1635 : " The governour and deputy were elected by papers wherein their names were written; but the assistants were chosen by papers, without names, viz: the governour propounded one to the people ; then they all went out, and came in at one door, and every man delivered a paper into a hat. Such as gave their vote for the party named, gave in a paper with some figures or scroll in it ; others gave in a blank." This seems to indicate that only those freemen who were present cast votes for the assistants at least. The next step was taken under Vane's administration, when it was voted March 9, 1636–7 (*Mass. Rec.* I, 188), that " it shall be free and lawful for all freemen to send their votes for elections by proxy the next General Court in May, and so for hereafter, which shall be done in this manner : The deputies which shall be chosen shall cause the freemen of their towns to be assembled, and then to take such freemen's votes as please to send by proxy for every magistrate, and seal them up, severally subscribing the magistrate's name on the back side, and so bring them to the Court sealed, with an open roll of the names of the freemen that so send by proxy."

In November, 1639 (*Mass. Rec.* I, 277), "it was solemnly and unanimously decreed and established that henceforth upon the day or days appointed by our patent to hold our yearly court for the electing of our Governor, Deputy Governor, Assistants and other general officers, being the last Wednesday of every Easter term, that the freemen of this jurisdiction shall, either in person or by proxy, without any summons, attend and consummate the elections; at which time also they shall send their deputies with full power to consult and determine such matters as concern the welfare of this Commonwealth : from which General Court no magistrate or deputy shall depart the Court, or be discharged, without the consent of the major part of the Court, under the penalty of one hundred pounds.

" As for the place of public assembling, it shall be where the preceding Court of Elections was held, unless then and there some other place shall be assigned. This act of ours we conceive so nearly to concern the good of this country, that we earnestly entreat it may never be repealed by any future Court."

On May 13th, 1640 (*Mass. Rec.* I, 293), it was ordered, that at the town meetings at which the deputies to the general court were chosen, these deputies should nominate to the freemen the candidates they recommended for the next election of magistrates, and should record the votes given to each candidate. The magistrates and deputies were to add the returns from the several towns, and take enough of these names according to the number of votes, to make up the full number of assistants. This list was to be returned to the freemen in each town to choose or reject at the next election; but no new name could be added to those nominated. This plan was to be tried for one year.

In June, 1641 (*Mass. Rec.* I, 333), it was ordered that the freemen in each town should choose electors to be sent to the court of election, one for every ten voters, who should have power to make election for all the rest.

In June, 1642 (*Mass. Rec.* II, 21), it was ordered that each town should send one or two freemen to Salem to agree upon a certain number of the most able and fit men to be put in nomination for magistrates at the next court, and none others were to be voted for.

In 1643, May 10 (*Rec.* II, 37), the mode appointed May 13, 1640, was revived until repealed or altered, except that it was declared that at the preliminary nominations in town meetings, the deputies should have no exclusive right of nominating, but all the freemen might propound names. September 7, 1643, it was ordered that the voting for assistants be with Indian beans, black and white, instead of papers.

On the 7th March, 1643–4, it was voted (*Rec.* II, 58), that the magistrates and deputies should thereafter sit apart, the assent of both houses being necessary to the passage of laws, &c. On the 13th November, 1644 (*Rec.* II, 87), it was ordered that within two months the freemen of each town should meet and select seven candidates for new magistrates at the next election. The town votes were then to be sent, sealed, to the shire towns by messengers on the last Thursday of February, and then these selected men for each county were to choose one to carry the sealed vote of the county to Boston, on the last Tuesday of March. At Boston, two magistrates were to open the votes and announce the seven names receiving the most votes, and "that such as have most votes to be first nominated and put to election, that the freemen may know for whom to send in their proxies." The county representatives were to notify the town messengers, and these latter the freemen, and none but the candidates thus proposed could be voted for.

This order, changing only the dates of the meeting in the shire towns, was renewed November 4, 1646 (*Rec.* III, 86).

In 1647, November 11 (*Rec.* II, 210), the same order was reenacted, with the important change that the number of nominees should be " to the number of seven persons, *or as the General Court shall direct*," and "these seven or other number agreed upon as aforesaid," should be nominated for assistants at the court of election.

On the 11th November, 1647 (*Rec.* II, 220), it was ordered that the freemen should elect the governor, deputy governor, major-general, treasurer, secretary, and commissioners for the United Colonies, by means of papers, and all the assistants by white beans, to be forwarded by their deputies to the court of election, "provided that such as are made free upon the day of election, and only they, shall deliver their votes at the door," and also provided that the votes of small villages which did not send deputies, should be transmitted by the deputies of the nearest town. This order apparently (see *Winthrop*, II, 311, old ed.), was not liked, since it made compulsory what was before optional, the voting by ballot. He seems to state that the order was repealed and the matter referred to the next court, 1648, which being full of business, the matter was put off farther.

Thus far the details of the elections seems to agree with Lechford's account in 1642 (*Plain Dealing*, p. 60, Trumbull's ed.), that at the election in Boston all the freemen voted in person or by proxy. He says, however, for the assistants the blanks and marked votes were counted, and "according to the major part of either, the man in nomination stands elected or rejected."

Considering the wording of these laws and the fact that from 1644 to 1649 there were at least ten assistants chosen each year, we feel obliged to conclude: 1st. That the governor, &c., were chosen by popular vote, by the freemen present at the meeting and by ballots sent thither. 2d. That the old assistants were renominated each year as a matter of course and voted on, whilst new names were propounded in accordance with these various schemes before cited, and only used if there were not enough old members desiring or attaining election to make up the number decided upon. It must be remembered that the number of assistants demanded by the charter, eighteen, was never filled before 1680, and it is believed that no evidence remains as to the mode by which the number to be elected in each year was decided upon, or as to the influence which determined this point.

On the 17th October, 1649 (*Rec.* II, 287), a new rule was made, viz: that on some day in November the freemen in each town were to cast their votes for such as they desired to have chosen assistants at the next court of election, not exceeding twenty in number (each freeman giving only one vote to each of his candidates); these votes were to be sent to the shire towns, and thence the county votes were to be sent to Boston. The eighteen having the most votes were to be the only candidates at the next election. They were to be nominated in the order of their relative votes, the highest first, "except such of those twenty who have been magistrates the year before, who shall have the precedence of the others in nomination on the day of election." "And the printed law for election, p. 21, bearing date 1647, is hereby repealed."

In support of this view we may note that the old assistants were regularly reelected from 1643 to 1649, and that though three were changed in 1650, viz: John Winthrop, jr., Saltonstall and Pelham, the first had removed to Connecticut, and the latter two had gone to England.

On the 19th October, 1658 (*Rec.* IV, part i, p. 347), it was ordered that inconveniences having arisen from having so many persons nominated, that hereafter only fourteen be nominated, and the previous law was repealed.

In 1665 (*Rec.* IV, part ii, p. 166), a letter was received from King Charles II, saying "although we have hereby declared our expectation to be that the charter granted by our royal father and now confirmed by us, shall be punctually observed, yet if the number of the Assistants enjoyned thereby by found by experience and by judged by the people to be inexpedient (as we are informed it is), we do then dispense with the same, and declare our will and pleasure herein for the future to be, that the number of said Assistants shall not exceed eighteen, nor be less at any time than ten."

October 12, 1670 (*Rec.* IV, part ii, p. 468), the number of nominees was fixed at eighteen.

Finally, 4 February, 1679–80 (*Rec.* v, 262), it was ordered that eighteen assistants be chosen for that year, and October 13, 1680 (*Rec.* v, 291), a more extended act was passed. The freemen of each town were to meet on the second Tuesday in March and vote by ballot for assistants to the number of twenty, casting only one vote for each candidate. Those votes were to be sent to the shire town, and thence by commissioners the county votes were to be carried to Boston. There on the 2d Tuesday in April the votes were to be opened, and the twenty-six having the most votes were to be the candidates for the next election. These nominees were to be considered according to the number of votes they had received, the old magistrates having the preference in nomination on election day. At the town meetings thereafter all the freemen might put in proxies for officers by ballots and Indian corn, naming twenty out of the twenty-six nominated for assistants, and these votes were to be sent to Boston, when the eighteen having the most votes were chosen for the next year. All the freemen who had not voted by proxy could do so in person on election day, at the Court House in Boston.

FIRST CHARTER.

GOVERNORS.		DEPUTY GOVERNORS.
1629 Oct. 20,	John Winthrop.*	John Humphrey.
1630†	do	Thomas Dudley.†
1631 May 18,	do	do
1632 May 9,	do	do
1633 May 29,	do	do
1634 May 14,	Thomas Dudley.	Roger Ludlow.
1635 May 6,	John Haynes.	Richard Bellingham.
1636 May 25,	Henry Vane.	John Winthrop.
1637 May 17,	John Winthrop.	Thomas Ludley.
1638 May 2,	do	do
1639 May 22,	do	do
1640 May 13,	Thomas Dudley.	Richard Bellingham.
1641 June 2,	Richard Bellingham.	John Endecott.
1642 May 18,	John Winthrop.	do
1643 May 10,	do	do
1644 May 29,	John Endecott,	John Winthrop.
1645 May 14,	Thomas Dudley.	do
1646 May 6,	John Winthrop.	Thomas Dudley.
1647 May 26,	do	do
1648 May 10,	do	do
1649 May 2,	John Endecott.	do
1650 May 22,	Thomas Dudley.	John Endecott.
1651 May 7,	John Endecott.	Thomas Dudley.
1652 May 27,	do	do
1653 May 18,	do	Richard Bellingham.
1654 May 3,	Richard Bellingham.	John Endecott.
1655 May 23,	John Endecott.	Richard Bellingham.
1656 May 14,	do	do
1657 May 6,	do	do
1658 May 19,	do	do
1659 May 11,	do	do
1660 May 30,	do	do
1661 May 22,	do	do
1662 May 7,	do	do
1663 May 27,	do	do
1664 May 18,	do	do
1665 May 3,	Richard Bellingham.	Francis Willoughby.
1666 May 23,	do	do
1667 May 15,	do	do

First Charter—Continued.

GOVERNORS.		DEPUTY GOVERNORS.
1668 Apr. 29,	Richard Bellingham.	Francis Willoughby.
1669 May 19,	do	do
1670 May 11,	do	do
1671 May 31,	do	John Leverett.
1672 May 15,	do	do
1673 May 7,	John Leverett.	Samuel Symonds.
1674 May 27,	do	do
1675 May 12,	do	do
1676 May 3,	do	do
1677 May 23,	do	do
1678 May 8,	do	do
1679 May 28,	Simon Bradstreet.	Thomas Danforth.
1680 May 19,	do	do
1681 May 11,	do	do
1682 May 24,	do	do
1683 May 16,	do	do
1684 May 7,	do	do
1685 May 27,	do	do
1686 May 12,	do	do

The general court adjourned May 20, 1686, the government being superseded by the new commission.

In 1684 proceedings were taken in England to vacate the charter, and a decree was finally issued October 23. A temporary government, directly dependent on the Crown, was projected by King Charles II, and Col. Piercy Kirk was appointed "His Majesty's Lieutenant and Governor General," early in November. During 1685 the old elective government continued, but was regarded only as provisional. On the 14th May, 1686, official information was brought to Boston of the new commissions issued by James II for the territory composed of Massachusetts, New Hampshire, Maine and the King's Province. The government was to consist of the president, deputy president, and sixteen counsellors. The commission is dated October 8, 1685.*

*Palfrey, III, 485.

3

DATE.	NAME.
1686	May 20,	Joseph Dudley, *President.*
"	William Stoughton, *Deputy President.*

1686	Dec. 20,	Sir Edmond Andros, *Governor.* He was appointed governor in chief over New England June 3, 1686, and assumed the authority on his arrival in December.
1688	April 7,	Andros was created by a new commission governor of all the English possessions on the main land of America, except Pennsylvania, Delaware, Maryland and Virginia.
1689	April 18,	Andros's government was overthrown, and a provisional government was established. Two conventions were called, which met May 9th and May 22d, and finally the old magistrates consented to assume office, though disclaiming the idea that they reassumed the old charter.
1689	May 24,	Simon Bradstreet, *Governor.* Thomas Danforth, *Deputy Governor.* This temporary government was sanctioned by William and Mary, and lasted till the arrival of the new or second charter, May 14, 1692.

SECRETARY.

1628-9, March 9, John Washborne was chosen secretary of the company in England for one year. 1629, May 13, William Burges was chosen, and the records are in his hand writing until 10 February, 1629-30. Simon Bradstreet's records commence March 18th, 1629-30, with the record of a meeting of the assistants at Southampton, and he doubtless was appointed at that time, though the earliest notice of his election is in 1634. The secretary held office for one year and until his successor was elected.

1630		Simon Bradstreet.
1636	June,	Increase Nowell. (He appears as acting secretary, though not formally elected until 1639).
1650	May 22,	Edward Rawson. (He held office until the charter was taken away).

| 1685 | Sept. 21, | Edward Randolph commissioned secretary and registrar under Dudley's government. He held until the overthrow of Andros in 1689. May 3, 1687 he rented his office to John West, who had acted as deputy under him. |

TREASURER.

The treasurers held office for one year and until their successors were appointed.

DATE.		NAME.	
1629	May 13,	George Harwood,	} In England.
1629	Dec. 1,	Samuel Aldersey,	
1632	Aug. 7,	William Pynchon.	
1634	May 18,	William Coddington.	
1636	May 25,	Richard Dummer.	
1637	May 17,	Richard Bellingham.	
1640	May 13,	William Tyng.	
1644	Nov. 13,	Richard Russell (until the next court).	
1645	May 14,	do	
1676	May 3,	John Hull.	
1680	May 19,	James Russell.	
1686	May 11,	Samuel Nowell.	

1686 June 1, John Usher, appointed under Dudley.

ASSISTANTS.

By the charter, eighteen assistants were to be chosen annually, but as has been noted (p. 14), this rule was continuously neglected for nearly fifty years. Until 1680 the number varied from seven to twelve, and we are at a loss to explain the reason of this palpable violation of the law. Hutchinson (*Hist.* I, 326), writes, under date of 1679 : "They continued to limit themselves to eight or ten assistants. At first, as has been observed, it was done to leave room for persons of quality expected from England. These expectations had long ceased. In a popular government, and where the magistrates were annually chosen, increasing the number would give a better chance to aspiring men. On the other hand, the greater the number of assistants the less the weight of the house of deputies, the election of all officers depending upon the major vote of the whole court. This last reason might cause the deputies to refuse their consent to an increase."

Finally, the king's letter of July 24, 1679 (*Hutchinson* I, 326), amongst other articles ordered that "the ancient number of eighteen assistants be henceforth observed as by charter." Accordingly at the session of 4th February, 1679–80, it was ordered by the court that for the future eighteen should be elected, twenty being voted for, and the eighteen receiving the most votes being declared elected (*Mass. Records*, V, 262).

At first the governor, deputy governor and assistants seem to have sat with the deputies, though exercising by a majority vote among themselves a negative upon the proceedings of the latter.   This privilege created dissension (*Hutchinson*, I, 143), and finally the deputies voted, 7th March, 1643–4, that the magistrates should sit by themselves.   The powers of the two bodies, however, seems to have remained quite undefined in theory.   In 1645, '6 and '7, the assistants were as before present at the court of elections, but after this last date they seem to have held separate sessions.

NOTES.—The following facts may be here noted :

1638.   John Endecott acted, but I do not find the date of his election.

1642.   The earlier copies of the published records were imperfect in regard to the elections this year.   Later copies, however, have a cancel of the first sheet, and two pages of additional matter are given, which supply the names recorded in the following list.   (See *Palfrey*, I, 613).

1652.   I do not find that Thomas Flynt was chosen this year, and as his will, of 21 December, 1651 (according to *Savage*), mentions that he was " intending a voyage to England," probably he went in 1652, and hence was not elected in his absence.

1685.   Oliver Purchase was elected, but declined.

ASSISTANTS.

[The governor and deputy governor in each year are marked with stars, but are not counted among the assistants. A star *prefixed* to a name shows that it has not occurred previously.]

NAMES.	1630	1631	1632	1633	1634
John Winthrop,	*	*	*	*	1
Thomas Dudley,	*	*	*	*	*
Increase Nowell,	1	1	1	1	1
Simon Bradstreet,	1	1	1	1	1
William Pynchon,	1	1	1	1	1
John Endecott,	1	1	1	1	1
William Coddington,	1	1	1	1	1
Roger Ludlow,	1	1	1	1	*
Sir Richard Saltonstall,	1	1	–	1	–
Isaac Johnson,	1	–	–	–	–
Thomas Sharp,	1	–	–	–	–
William Vassall,	1	–	–	–	–
Edward Rossiter,	1	–	–	–	–
John Winthrop, jr.,	–	–	1	1	1
John Humfrey,	–	–	1	1	1
John Haynes,	–	–	–	–	1
	11	7	8	9	9

NAMES.	1635	1636	1637	1638	1639
John Winthrop,	1	*	*	*	*
Thomas Dudley,	1	1	*	*	*
Increase Nowell,	1	1	1	1	1
Simon Bradstreet,	1	1	1	1	1
William Pynchon,	1	1	–	–	–
John Endecott,	–	1	1	1	1
William Coddington,	1	1	–	–	–
John Winthrop, jr.,	1	1	1	1	1
John Haynes,	*	1	–	–	–
*Richard Bellingham,	*	1	1	1	1
*Richard Dummer,	1	1	–	–	–
John Humfrey,	1	1	1	1	1
*Atherton Hough,	1	–	–	–	–
*Roger Harlakenden,	–	1	1	1	–
*Sir Henry Vane,	–	*	–	–	–
*Israel Stoughton,	–	–	1	1	1
*Richard Saltonstall, jr.,	–	–	1	1	1
	10	12	9	9	8

Assistants—Continued.

NAMES.	1640	1641	1642	1643	1644	1645
John Winthrop, . .	1	1	*	*	*	*
Thomas Dudley, . .	*	1	1	1	1	*
Increase Nowell, . .	1	1	1	1	1	1
Simon Bradstreet, . .	1	1	1	1	1	1
John Endecott, . .	1	*	*	*	*	1
John Winthrop, jr., .	1	1	1	1	1	1
Richard Bellingham, .	*	*	1	1	1	1
John Humfrey, . .	1	1	–	–	–	–
Israel Stoughton, . .	1	1	1	1	–	–
Richard Saltonstall, jr., .	1	1	1	1	1	1
*Thomas Flint, . .	–	–	1	1	1	1
*Samuel Symonds, . .	–	–	–	1	1	1
*William Hibbens, .	–	–	–	1	1	1
*William Pynchon, .	–	–	1	1	1	1
*Herbert Pelham, .	–	–	–	–	–	1
	8	8	9	11	10	11

NAMES.	1646	1647	1648	1649
John Winthrop, ...	*	*	*	–
Thomas Dudley, ...	*	*	*	*
Increase Nowell, . . .	1	1	1	1
Simon Bradstreet, . . .	1	1	1	1
John Endecott, . . .	1	1	1	*
William Pynchon, . . .	1	1	1	1
Richard Bellingham, . .	1	1	1	1
John Winthrop, jr., . .	1	1	1	1
Richard Saltonstall, jr., .	1	1	1	1
Thomas Flint, . . .	1	1	1	1
Samuel Symonds, . .	1	1	1	1
William Hibbens, . .	1	1	1	1
Herbert Pelham, . .	1	1	1	1
*Robert Bridges, . .	–	1	1	1
	11	12	12	11

Assistants—Continued.

NAMES.	1650	1651	1652	1653	1654	1655
Thomas Dudley,	*	*	*	—	—	
Increase Nowell,	1	1	1	1	1	1
Simon Bradstreet,	1	1	1	1	1	1
John Endecott,	*	*	*	*	*	*
William Pynchon,	1	—	—	—	—	—
Richard Bellingham,	1	1	1	*	*	*
Thomas Flint,	1	1	—	1	—	—
Samuel Symonds,	1	1	1	1	1	1
William Hibbens,	1	1	1	1	1	—
Robert Bridges,	1	1	1	1	1	1
*Francis Willoughby,	1	1	—	—	—	
*Edward Gibbons,	1	1	—	—	—	—
*Thomas Wiggin,	1	1	1	1	1	1
*John Glover,	—	—	1	1	—	—
*Daniel Gookin,	—	—	1	1	1	1
*Daniel Denison,	—	—	—	1	1	1
*Simon Willard,	—	—	—	—	1	1
*Humphrey Atherton,	—	—	—	—	1	1
	11	10	9	10	10	9

NAMES.	1656	1657	1658	1659	1660	1661
Richard Bellingham,	*	*	*	*	*	*
John Endecott,	*	*	*	*	*	*
Simon Bradstreet,	1	1	1	1	1	1
Samuel Symonds,	1	1	1	1	1	1
Robert Bridges,	1	—	—	—	—	—
Thomas Wiggin,	1	1	1	1	1	1
Daniel Gookin,	1	1	1	1	1	1
Daniel Denison,	1	1	1	1	1	1
Simon Willard,	1	1	1	1	1	1
Humphrey Atherton,	1	1	1	1	1	1
*Richard Russell,	—	—	—	1	1	1
*Thomas Danforth,	—	—	—	1	1	1
	8	7	7	9	9	9

Assistants—Continued.

NAMES.	1662	1663	1664	1665	1666	1667
Richard Bellingham, .	*	*	*	*	*	*
John Endecott, . .	*	*	*	–	–	–
Simon Bradstreet, . .	1	1	1	1	1	1
Samuel Simonds, .	1	1	1	1	1	1
Thomas Wiggin, .	1	1	1	–	–	–
Daniel Gookin, .	1	1	1	1	1	1
Daniel Denison, .	1	1	1	1	1	1
Simon Willard, .	1	1	1	1	1	1
Richard Russell, .	1	1	1	1	1	1
Thomas Danforth, .	1	1	1	1	1	1
*William Hawthorne, .	1	1	1	1	1	1
*Eliezer Lusher, .	1	1	1	1	1	1
Francis Willoughby, .	–	–	1	*	*	*
Richard Saltonstall, jr. .	–	–	1	–	–	–
*John Leverett, .	–	–	–	1	1	1
*John Pynchon, .	–	–	–	1	1	1
	10	10	12	11	11	11

NAMES.	1668	1669	1670	1671	1672
Richard Bellingham, . .	*	*	*	*	*
Simon Bradstreet, . . .	1	1	1	1	1
Samuel Symonds, . . .	1	1	1	1	1
Daniel Gookin, . . .	1	1	1	1	1
Daniel Denison, . . .	1	1	1	1	1
Simon Willard, . . .	1	1	1	1	1
Richard Russell, . . .	1	1	1	1	1
Thomas Danforth, . . .	1	1	1	1	1
William Hawthorne, . . .	1	1	1	1	1
Eliezar Lusher, . . .	1	1	1	1	1
Francis Willoughby, . .	*	*	*	–	–
John Leverett, . . .	1	1	1	*	*
John Pynchon, . . .	1	1	1	1	1
*Edward Tyng, . . .	1	1	1	1	1
*William Stoughton, . .	–	–	–	1	1
	12	12	12	12	12

Assistants—Continued.

NAMES.	1673	1674	1675	1676
Simon Bradstreet,	1	1	1	1
Samuel Symonds,	*	*	*	*
Daniel Gookin,	1	1	1	–
Daniel Denison,	1	1	1	1
Simon Willard,	1	1	1	–
Richard Russell,	1	1	1	1
Thomas Danforth,	1	1	1	1
William Hawthorne,	1	1	1	1
John Leverett,	*	*	*	*
John Pynchon,	1	1	1	1
Edward Tyng,	1	1	1	1
William Stoughton,	1	1	1	1
*Thomas Clarke,	1	1	1	1
*Joseph Dudley,	–	–	–	1
	11	11	11	10

NAMES.	1677	1678	1679
Simon Bradstreet,	1	1	*
Samuel Symonds,	*	*	–
Daniel Gookin,	1	1	1
Daniel Denison,	1	1	1
Thomas Danforth,	1	1	*
William Hawthorne,	1	1	1
John Leverett,	*	*	
John Pynchon,	1	1	1
Edward Tyng,	1	1	1
William Stoughton,	1	1	1
Thomas Clarke,	1	–	–
Joseph Dudley,	1	1	1
*Peter Bulkley,	1	1	1
*Nathaniel Saltonstall,	–	–	1
*Humphrey Davy,	–	–	1
	10	10	10

4

Assistants—Continued.

NAMES.	1680	1681	1682	1683	1684	1685	1686
Simon Bradstreet,	*	*	*	*	*	*	*
Thomas Danforth,	*	*	*	*	*	*	*
Daniel Gookin,	1	1	1	1	1	1	1
Daniel Denison,	1	1	1	–	–	–	–
John Pynchon,	1	1	1	1	1	1	1
Edward Tyng,	1	–	–	–	–	–	–
William Stoughton,	1	1	1	1	1	1	1
Joseph Dudley,	1	1	1	1	–	1	–
Peter Bulkley,	1	1	1	1	1	–	–
Nathaniel Saltonstall,	1	1	1	1	1	1	1
Humphrey Davy,	1	1	1	1	1	1	1
*James Russell,	1	1	1	1	1	1	1
*Samuel Nowell,	1	1	1	1	1	1	1
*Peter Tilton,	1	1	1	1	1	1	1
*John Richards,	1	1	1	1	1	1	1
Richard Saltonstall, jr.,	1	1	1	–	–	–	–
*John Hull,	1	1	1	1	–	–	–
*Bartholomew Gedney,	1	1	1	1	–	–	–
*Thomas Savage,	1	1	–	–	–	–	–
*William Browne,	1	1	1	1	–	–	–
*Samuel Appleton,	–	1	1	1	1	1	1
*Robert Pike,	–	–	1	1	1	1	1
*Daniel Fisher,	–	–	–	1	–	–	–
*John Woodbridge,	–	–	–	1	1	–	–
*Elisha Cooke,	–	–	–	–	1	1	1
*William Johnson,	–	–	–	–	1	1	1
*John Hawthorne,	–	–	–	–	1	1	1
*Elisha Hutchinson,	–	–	–	–	1	1	1
*Samuel Sewall,	–	–	–	–	1	1	1
*Isaac Addington,	–	–	–	–	–	–	1
*John Smith,	–	–	–	–	–	–	1
*Oliver Purchase,†	–	–	–	–	–	0	–
	18	18	18	18	18	17	18

† Declined.

SPEAKER OF THE HOUSE OF DEPUTIES.

The first record of the appointment of this officer is at the session beginning May 29, 1644, after the separation of the assistants and deputies. Before this time we may conclude that the governor presided. The speaker was chosen anew at each session of the court.

1644 May 29, William Hawthorne.	1665 May 3, Thomas Clarke.
1645 May 14, do	1666 May 23, Richard Waldron.
Aug. 12, do	1667 May 15, do
Oct. 2, George Cooke.	1668 Apr. 29, do
1646 May 6, William Hawthorne.	1669 May 19, Thomas Clarke.
Nov. 4, Robert Bridges,	1670 May 11, do
1647 May 26, Joseph Hill.	1671 May 31, Thomas Savage.
Oct. 18, Richard Russell.	1672 May 15, Thomas Clarke.
1648 May 10, William Hawthorne.	1673 May 7, Richard Waldron.
Oct. 18, Richard Russell.	1673–4 Jan. 6, Josh. Hubbard.
1649 May 2, Daniel Denison.	1674 May 27, Richard Waldron.
Oct. 17, do	1674 Oct. 7, do
1650 May 23, William Hawthorne.	1675 May 12, do
Oct. 15, do	1675–6 Feb. 21, Peter Bulkley.
1651 May 7, Daniel Gookin.	1676 May 3, do
Oct. 14, Daniel Denison.	Aug. 9, do
1652 May 27, do	1677 May 24, Thomas Savage.
1653 May 18, Humphrey Atherton.	Oct. 10, do
1654 May 3, Richard Russell.	1678 May 9, do
1655 May 23, Edward Johnson.	1679 May 28, Richard Waldron.
1656 May 14, Richard Russell.	1679–80 Feb. 4, John Richards.
1657 May 6, William Hawthorne.	1680 May 19, Daniel Fisher.
1658 May 19, Richard Russell.	1681 May 11, do
1659 May 11, Thomas Savage.	1682 May 24, do
1660 May 30, do	1683 May 16, Elisha Cooke.
1661 May 22, William Hawthorne.	Nov. 7, do
1662 May 7, Thomas Clarke.	1684 May 7, John Wayt.
1663 May 27, John Leverett.	1685 May 27, Isaac Addington.
1664 May 18, do	1686 May 12, John Satlin,

COMMISSIONERS OF THE UNITED COLONIES.

(Elected at the Annual Election in each Colony.)

	MASSACHUSETTS.		PLYMOUTH.	
1643	John Winthrop,	Thomas Dudley,	Edward Winslow,	William Collier,
1644	Simon Bradstreet,	Wm. Hathorne,	do	John Browne,
1645	John Winthrop,	Herbert Pelham,	Thomas Prince,	do
1646	John Endecott,	do	Timothy Hatherley,	do
1647	do	Thomas Dudley,	William Bradford,	do
1648	do	Simon Bradstreet,	do	do
1649	Thomas Dudley,	do	do	do
1650	Wm. Hathorne,	do	Thomas Prince,	do
1651	do	do	Timothy Hatherley,	do
1652	do	do	William Bradford,	do
1653	do	do	Thomas Prence,	do
1654	do	do	do	do
1655	Daniel Denison,	do	do	do
1656	do	do	do	William Bradford,
1657	do	do	do	James Cudworth,
1658	John Endecott,	do	do	Josias Winslow,
1659	Daniel Denison,	do	Thomas Southworth,	do
1660	do	do	do	do
1661	do	do	do	Thomas Prence,
1662	do	Thomas Danforth,	Josias Winslow,	T. Southworth,
1663	Simon Bradstreet,	do	do	Thomas Prence,
1664	do	do	do	T. Southworth,
1665	do	do	do	do
1666	do	do	do	do
1667	*	do	do	do
1668	Thomas Danforth,	John Leverett,	Josias Winslow,	do
1669	do	do	do	do
1670	do	Simon Bradstreet,	do	Thomas Prence,
1671	do	do	do	do
1672	do	do	do	do
1673	do	Wm. Hathorne,	do	Thos. Hinckley,
1674	do	Wm. Stoughton,	do	do
1675	do	do	do	do

* John Leverett in reserve seems to have acted this year.   † James Cudworth, substitute, served.

Commissioners of the United Colonies—Continued.

	MASSACHUSETTS.		PLYMOUTH.	
1676	Thos. Danforth,	Wm. Stoughton,	Josias Winslow,	Thomas Hinckley,
1677	do	Joseph Dudley,	do	do
1678	do	do	do	do
1679	do	do	do	do
1680	Wm. Stoughton,	do	do	do
1681	do	do	James Cudworth,	do
1682	do	Peter Bulkley,	William Bradford,	do
1683	do	do	do	do
1684	do	Samuel Nowell,	do	do
1685	do	do		
1686	do	do	do	do

NOTE.—Usually substitutes were also chosen, and these sometimes acted. Thus, for Massachusetts John Leverett acted in 1667, and for Plymouth, Thomas Prence in 1662, and Thomas Hinckley in 1667.

INTER CHARTER PERIOD.

(See *Palfrey*, III, 604).

---

*JOSEPH DUDLEY, President in 1686.
*WILLIAM STOUGHTON, Deputy President in 1686.

COUNSELLORS.

*Robert Mason,
*Fitz John Winthrop,
*John Pynchon,
*Peter Bulkley,
*Edward Randolph,
*Wait Still Winthrop,
*Richard Wharton,
*John Usher,

*Bartholomew Gedney,
*Jonathan Tyng,
*John Hinckes,
*Edward Tyng,
Nathaniel Saltonstall,†
Simon Bradstreet,†
Dudley Bradstreet,†
Francis Champernoon.†

In Andros's first commission the above twelve marked with stars were reappointed, and the following thirteen added :

Thomas Hinckley,
Barnabas Lothrop,
William Bradford,
Daniel Smith,
John Walley,
Nathaniel Clarke,
John Coggeshall,

Walter Clark,
Walter Newberry,
John Sanford,
John Greene,
Richard Arnold,
John Albro.

These were all in office from 1686 to 1689, and the following four were added at the dates named :

Francis Nicholson, August, 1687,
Robert Treat, November, 1687,

John Allyn, November, 1687.
Samuel Shrimpton, March, 1688.

---

† Did not accept.

In Andros's second Commission (April 16, 1688), forty-two members of the council are named (*N. Y. Doc.* III, 543), viz : all the foregoing (except the four who did not accept), and

William Browne,	Stephen Van Courtlandt,*
Richard Smith,	John Young.
Simond Lynde,	Nicholas Bayard,
Anthony Brockholst,	John Palmer,
Frederick Phillips,	John Sprague,
Jarvis Baxter.*	

This council was of course dispersed at Andros's overthrow.

The following names were signed April 18th, 1689, to the demand for Andros's surrender :

Wait Winthrop,	Elisha Cooke,
Simon Bradstreet,	Isaac Addington,
William Stoughton,	John Nelson,
Samuel Shrimpton,	Adam Winthrop,
Bartholomew Gedney,	Peter Sergeant,
William Brown,	John Foster,
Thomas Danforth,	David Waterhouse.
John Richards,	

On the 20th April the above, together with the following, formed a "Council for the safety of the people, and conservation of the peace." (*Hutchinson*, I, 381-2).

James Russell,	Andrew Belcher,
John Phillips,	Richard Sprague,
Penn Townsend,	James Parker,
Joseph Lynde,	Dudley Bradstreet,
John Joyliffe,	Nathaniel Saltonstall,
Eliakim Hutchinson,	Richard Dummer,
Nathaniel Oliver,	Robert Pike,
John Eyre,	John Smith,
Jeremiah Dummer,	Edmund Quincy,
William Johnson,	William Bond,
John Hathorne,	Daniel Pierce.

They chose Bradstreet, President; John Foster and Adam Winthrop, Treasurers; Wait Winthrop, Commander-in-Chief; Isaac Addington, Clerk.

---

* NOTE.—*Palfrey* has Anthony Baxter and Henry Courtland in place of these two, but the names are plainly given in the record, and are those of prominent men in New York. On the other hand, the record says *John* Nicholson, though undoubtedly Francis Nicholson, the lieutenant governor, is meant.

Inter Charter Period—Continued.

May 22, 1689, representatives of fifty-four towns met at Boston, and the governor (Bradstreet), and assistants chose in 1686, reassumed office provisionally, the other members of the council of safety resigning. This government lasted until the new charter was obtained.

NOTE.—From the records at the state house of Dudley's brief administration in 1686, we take the following items:

1686. May 25, Giles Dyer appointed receiver of duties on wines and liquors imported.

May 28, John Usher treasurer; Mr. Nowell late treasurer; Richard Bulkley clerk to take account and give license to ship horses; Nathaniel Barnes was his predecessor.

John Green, marshal of Middlesex.

May 29, Francis Hooke, to take account of wines, &c., imported into York and Kittery; Robert Estwick, for the rest of the province.

June 2, Officers appointed:

FOR SUFFOLK.

Daniel Allen, } *Clerks.*   John Winchcomb, } *Marshals.*
Thomas Dudley,   Nathaniel Page,
John Blake, *Coroner.*

FOR ESSEX.

Samuel Sewall, *Clerk.*   Jeremiah Neal, *Marshal.*
Samuel Gardner, *Coroner.*

FOR HAMPSHIRE.

John Holyoke, } *Clerks.*   Samuel Marshfield, *Marshal.*
Samuel Partridge,   Joseph Hawley, *Coroner.*

FOR THE PROVINCE OF NEW HAMPSHIRE.

Richard Chamberlain, *Clerk.*   Pheasant Estwick, *Coroner.*
June 3, Major Bulkeley, *Provost Marshal.*
Capt. Edward Tyng, to have command of Fort Loyall.
June 8, Nicholas Manning, marshal of Falmouth and vicinity.
June 17, Thomas Scottow, clerk of the province of Maine, in place of Edward Rushworth.

July 12, Pheasant Eastwick, marshal of New Hampshire.
    20, Jonathan Hammond, marshal of Maine.
    21, John Richards and Simon Lynde, to assist in holding county courts for Suffolk, until further order.
    22, Thomas Davey, coroner for Hampshire.
    23, Daniel Cheevers, keeper of the gaol in Middlesex.
    26, John Richards and Simon Lynde, judges of the next court of pleas at Boston.

John Hincks, one of the council at Great Island, to be captain of the fort there, and of the train band.

Richard Waldron, jr., to be clerk of the court and probate, paying £10 yearly to Richard Chamberlain ;. also, deputy register to Edward Randolph, in New Hampshire, on the same terms that Mr. Scotto is in Maine.

William Stoughton, empowered to take charge of the several courts in Suffolk, Middlesex and Essex.

    5

AUDITOR GENERAL.

This office was created 18th October, 1645, and abolished 23d October, 1657. The only incumbent seems to have been '
            Nathaniel Duncan.

MARSHAL GENERAL.

1636.   James Penn.
1637.   Edward Mitchelson (who held undoubtedly till 1681).
1681.   May 27, John Greene was appointed.

AGENTS SENT TO ENGLAND.

1641.   June 2, Rev. Hugh Peter, Rev. Thomas Welde, and William Hibbens were appointed "to go for England upon some weighty occasions for the good of the country, as was conceived." John Winthrop, jr., accompanied them. Their agency terminated 1 October, 1645. John Pocock of London had been associated with them, and after their dismissal remained in charge until Winslow's arrival. (*Palfrey* II, 176).

1646.   Edward Winslow.

1662. January, Simon Bradstreet and Rev. John Norton sent specially, who returned September 8th, 1662.

1676.   Sept'r, William Stoughton and Peter Bulkley sent. They arrived home December 23d, 1679.

1681.   March, Samuel Nowell and John Richards chosen, Stoughton declining a second appointment. Nowell also declined, and a new choice was made.

1682.   Joseph Dudley and John Richards were chosen, and sailed 31st May. They arrived back 23d October, 1683. Mr. Robert Humphreys, of London, appeared for the colony at the court of king's bench in the matter of the forfeiture of the charter.

1688.   April, Rev. Increase Mather went as an informal agent, there being no legislature under Andros. Sir Henry Ashurst acted with him.

1690.   Mather and Ashurst were appointed by the restored government, together with Elisha Cooke and Thomas Oakes.

PLYMOUTH.

GOVERNORS.

(The record only commences in 1634. The following facts are, however, certain).

DATE.	NAMES.	DATE.	NAMES.
1620–21,	John Carver,	1660, June 6,	Thomas Prence,
1621, May,	Wm. Bradford,*	1661, June 4,	do
1633–4, Jan. 1,	Thomas Prence,	1662, June 3,	do
1634–5, March 3,	Wm. Bradford,	1663, June 1,	do
1635–6, Jan. 5,	Edward Winslow,	1664, June 8,	do
1636–7, Jan. 3,	Wm. Bradford,	1665, June 7,	do
1638, June 5,	Thomas Prence,†	1666, June 5,	do
1638–9, March 5,	Wm. Bradford,	1667, June 5,	do
1639–40, M'ch 3,	do	1668, June 3,	do
1640–1, March 2,	do	1669, June 1,	do
1641–2, March 1,	do	1670, June 7,	do‖
1642–3, March 7,	do	1671, June 5,	do
1644, June 5,	Edward Winslow,	1672, June 5,	do
1645, June 4,	Wm. Bradford,	1673, June 3,	Josias Winslow,
1646,‡		1674, June 3,	do
1647, June 1,	do	1675, June 1,	do
1648, June 7,	do	1676, June 7,	do
1649,§		1677, June 5,	do
1650, June 4,	do	1678, June 5,	do
1651, June 5,	do	1679, June 3,	do
1652, June 3,	do	1680, June 1,	do
1653, June 7,	do	1681, June 7,	Thomas Hinckley,
1654, June 6,	do	1682, June 6,	do
1655, June 8,	do	1683, June 6,	do
1656, June 3,	do	1684, June 3,	do
1657, June 3,	Thomas Prence,	1685, June 2,	do
1658, June 1,	do	1686, June –,	do
1659, June 7,	do		

* Bradford continued in office until the election of Prence.

† 1638, at the March Meeting, Bradford and the assistants were continued until the next court. (*Rec.* 1, 80).

‡ No election for 1646 recorded.

§ No election. See *Rec.* 11, 139.

‖ 1670 (*Rec.* v, 55). "This court have ordered that if God should take away the governor by death, or otherwise deprive us of his health by absence, or other bodily weakness disable him to discharge his place, that in such case the next eldest magistrate is to serve in the office of a deputy governor for this present year, as the governor might and ought to do."

DEPUTY GOVERNORS.

DATE.	NAMES.	DATE.	NAMES.
1680, June 1,	Thomas Hinckley,	1684, June 3,	William Bradford,
1681, June 7,	James Cudworth,	1685, June 2,	do
1682, June 6,	William Bradford,	1686, June –,	do
1683, June 6,	do		

SECRETARY.

1636–7, January 3, Nathaniel Souther chosen clerk of the court.

1647, December 7, Nathaniel Morton, probably then chosen, as his records begin then. Held office till near his death, June 29, 1685.

1685,   June   2, Nathaniel Clarke chosen.

1686,   June   Samuel Sprague chosen.

1689,   June   do   chosen, and again in 1690 and 1691.

TREASURER.

1636–7, January 5, Thomas Prince.

1639–40, March 3, Timothy Hatherley.

1641–2,   March   1, John Atwood.

1644,   August 20, Miles Standish, and continued until

1656,   June   3, John Alden.

1659,   June   7, Constant Southworth, reelected until

1679,   June   3, William Bradford, reelected until 1686, when the government was dissolved.

1689,   June   William Bradford, and again in 1690.

ASSISTANTS.

The record commences in 1634, and from that time elections were annual. Before that, we learn from *Bradford's History* (p. 101), that Isaac Allerton was chosen assistant in 1621. In 1624 the number was raised to five, the governor having a double vote. In 1632 (p. 306, *note*), the editor says that Miles Standish, Samuel Fuller, John Alden and Thomas Prence probably held this office.

NAMES.	1624	1635	1636	1637	1638	1639
Isaac Allerton, . .	1	—	—	—	—	—
Edward Winslow, . .	1	1	—	1	1	—
William Bradford, . .	1	—	1	—	1	—
John Alden, . .	1	1	1	1	1	1
John Howland, . .	1	1	—	—	—	—
Stephen Hopkins, . .	1	1	1	—	—	—
Thomas Prence, . .	—	1	1	1	—	1
Miles Standish, . .	—	1	—	1	1	1
William Collier, . .	—	1	1	1	—	1
Timothy Hatherley, . .	—	—	1	1	—	1
John Browne, . .	—	—	1	—	1	1
John Jenney, . .	—	—	—	1	1	1
John Atwood, . .	—	—	—	—	1	—
	6	7	7	7	7	7

NAMES.	1640	1641	1642	1643	1644	1645
Edward Winslow, . .	—	1	1	1	—	1
Thomas Prence, . .	1	1	1	1	1	1
Miles Standish, . .	1	1	—	—	—	1
William Collier, . .	1	1	1	1	1	1
Timothy Hatherley, . .	1	1	1	1	1	1
John Browne, . .	1	1	1	1	1	1
John Jenney, . .	1	—	—	—	—	—
*Edmond Freeman, . .	1	1	1	1	1	1
*William Bradford, . .	—	—	—	—	1	—
*William Thomas, . .	—	—	1	1	1	—
	7	7	7	7	7	7

Assistants—Continued.

NAMES.	1646	1647	1648	1649	1650	1651
Edward Winslow, . .	1	1	1	1	1	–
Thomas Prence, . .	1	1	1	1	1	1
Miles Standish, . .	1	1	1	1	1	1
William Collier, . .	1	1	1	1	1	1
Timothy Hatherley, . .	1	1	1	1	1	1
John Browne, . .	1	1	1	1	1	1
William Thomas, . .	1	1	1	1	1	–
*John Alden, . .	–	–	–	–	1	1
*Thomas Willett, . .	–	–	–	–	–	1
	7	7	7	7	7	7

NAMES.	1652	1653	1654	1655	1656	1657
Thomas Prence, . .	1	1	1	1	1	–
Miles Standish, . .	1	1	1	1	1	–
William Collier, . .	–	–	1	1	1	1
Timothy Hatherley, . .	1	1	1	1	1	1
John Browne, . .	1	1	1	1	–	–
John Alden, . .	1	1	1	1	1	1
Thomas Willett, . .	1	1	1	1	1	1
James Cudworth, . .	–	–	–	–	1	1
*Josias Winslow, . .	–	–	–	–	–	1
*Thomas Southworth, .	–	–	–	–	–	1
	6	6	7	7	7	7

NAMES.	1658	1659	1660	1661	1662	1663
William Collier, . .	1	1	1	1	1	1
Timothy Hatherley, . .	1	–	–	–	–	–
John Alden, . .	1	1	1	1	1	1
Thomas Willett, . .	1	1	1	1	1	1
Josias Winslow, . .	1	1	1	1	1	1
Thomas Southworth, .	1	1	1	1	1	1
*William Bradford, . .	1	1	1	1	1	1
*Thomas Hinckley, . .	1	1	1	1	1	1
	8	7	7	7	7	7

NAMES.	1664	1665	1666	1667	1668	1669
William Collier, . .	1	1	–	–	–	–
John Alden, . .	1	1	1	1	1	1
Thomas Willett, . .	1	–	–	–	–	–
Josias Winslow, . .	1	1	1	1	1	1
Thomas Southworth, .	1	1	1	1	1	1
William Bradford, . .	1	1	1	1	1	1
Thomas Hinckley, . .	1	1	1	1	1	1
*John Freeman, . .	–	–	–	1	1	1
*Nathaniel Bacon, . .	–	–	–	1	1	1
	7	6	5	7	7	7

NAMES.	1670	1671	1672	1673	1674	1675
John Alden, . .	1	1	1	1	1	1
Josias Winslow, . .	1	1	1	–	–	–
Thomas Southworth, . .	1	1	–	–	–	–
William Bradford, . .	1	1	1	1	1	1
Thomas Hinckley, . .	1	1	1	1	1	1
John Freeman, . .	1	1	1	1	1	1
Nathaniel Bacon, . .	1	1	1	1	–	–
*Constant Southworth, .	–	–	1	1	1	1
*James Browne, . .	–	–	–	1	1	1
*James Cudworth, . .	–	–	–		1	1
	7	7	7	7	7	7

Assistants—Continued.

NAMES.	1676	1677	1678	1679	1680	1681
John Alden, . . .	1	1	1	1	1	1
William Bradford, . .	1	1	1	1	1	1
Thomas Hinckley, . .	1	1	1	1	–	–
John Freeman, . .	1	1	1	1	1	1
Constant Southworth, .	1	1	1	–	–	–
James Browne, .	1	1	1	1	1	1
James Cudworth, . .	1	1	1	1	1	–
*Daniel Smith, . .	–	–	–	1	1	1
*Barnabas Lothrop, . .	–	–	–	–	–	1
	7	7	7	7	6	6

NAMES.	1682	1683	1684	1685	1686
John Alden, . . .	1	1	1	1	1
John Freeman, . . .	1	1	1	1	1
James Browne, . . .	1	1	–	–	–
Daniel Smith, . . .	1	1	1	1	1
Barnabas Lothrop, . .	1	1	1	1	1
John Thatcher, . . .	1	1	1	1	1
John Walley, . . .	–	–	1	1	1
	6	6	6	6	6

NOTE.—In 1652 and 1653 Thomas Southworth was chosen but not sworn. March 29, 1654–5, he took the oath of an assistant to serve in that office at the river of Kennebec.

1665, James Browne, chosen but not sworn.

1666, James Browne and John Freeman chosen but not sworn.

LIST OF CIVIL OFFICERS
UNDER THE SECOND CHARTER,
OR
THE PROVINCIAL PERIOD.

GOVERNORS.

SIR WILLIAM PHIPS. Appointed October, 1691, and commissioned December 12, 1691. Arrived at Boston May 14, 1692. Our Council records commence May 16, 1692, probably the date of his entrance upon his duties. He left Boston November 17, 1694.

Lt. Gov. WILLIAM STOUGHTON.* November, 1694, till the arrival of Bellomont.

RICHARD, EARL OF BELLOMONT. Arrived at Boston May 26, 1699, and his commission was published that day. He went to New York in May, 1700, and died the 5th of March following. Commissioned June 18, 1697.

Lt. Gov. WILLIAM STOUGHTON.* From May, 1700, till his death, July 7, 1701.

THE COUNCIL. From July, 1701, till June, 1702.

JOSEPH DUDLEY. Arrived at Boston June 11, 1702. He acted till February 4, 1714-15, when the Council assumed control, Dudley not having been confirmed by the new king. Commissioned April 1, 1702.

THE COUNCIL. February 4, 1714-15, till March 21, 1714-15.

JOSEPH DUDLEY. March 21, 1714-15, the king's proclamation was read, and Dudley reassumed office.

COL. ELIZEUS OR ELISHA BURGESS. His commission passed the seals March 17, 1714-15, and was published at Boston November 9, 1715. He sold his commission to Col. Shute's friends for £1,000 in April, 1716.

Lt. Gov. WILLIAM TAILER.* Took the office November 9, 1715, and acted till the arrival of Shute.

SAMUEL SHUTE. He was appointed upon the 15th June, 1716, and arrived at Boston October 4, 1716. He left Boston suddenly January 1, 1722-3.

Lt. Gov. WILLIAM DUMMER.* From January 1, 1722-3, till the arrival of Burnet.

WILLIAM BURNET. He was appointed March 7, 1727-8, and arrived at Boston July 13, 1728. He died at Boston September 7, 1729.

Lt. Gov. WILLIAM DUMMER. Succeeded at Burnet's death, and sworn September 10 as commander-in-chief.

JONATHAN BELCHER. Commissioned January 8, 1729-30. Arrived at Boston August 10, 1730.

WILLIAM SHIRLEY. Commissioned May 16, 1741. He was then living at Boston. His administration ended at Pownall's arrival.

THOMAS POWNALL. Appointed February 25, 1757. Arrived at Boston August 2, 1757. He was transferred to South Carolina, and sailed for England June 3, 1760.

Lt. Gov. THOMAS HUTCHINSON.* From Pownall's departure till the arrival of Bernard.

SIR FRANCIS BERNARD. Commissioned January 14, 1760. Arrived at Boston August 2, 1760. Sailed for England August 2, 1769.

Lt. Gov. THOMAS HUTCHINSON.* From Bernard's departure till his own commission as governor arrived.

* Acting Governor.

THOMAS HUTCHINSON. Appointed November 28, 1770. His commission was received at the beginning of March, 1771. Superseded 1774. Sailed for England June 1, 1774.

Gen. THOMAS GAGE. Appointed April 7, 1774. Arrived in Boston May 13, 1774. In May, 1775, the Provincial Congress declared him disqualified from serving as Governor. In October, 1775, he sailed for England.

LIEUTENANT-GOVERNORS.

WILLIAM STOUGHTON. Appointed under the new charter, probably late in 1691. Continued in office till his death, June 7, 1701.

THOMAS POVEY. Appointed April 11, 1702. Arrived at Boston June 11, 1702. Returned to England in 1705.

WILLIAM TAILER. Appointed , 1711. Arrived October 3, 1711, and took the oaths October 4, 1711. Superseded by Dummer.

WILLIAM DUMMER. Appointed probably with Shute. He held office till superseded by Tailer.

WILLIAM TAILER. Appointed a second time April 14, 1730, and died in office March 1, 1731-2, aged 55.

SPENCER PHIPS. Appointed , 1733. Died in office April 4, 1757, aged 71.

THOMAS HUTCHINSON. Appointed January 31, 1758. Commission published in Council June 1, 1758. Became acting governor August, 1769, and was promoted to be governor.

ANDREW OLIVER. Succeeded Hutchinson in March, 1771. He died March 3, 1774.

THOMAS OLIVER. Appointed , 1774. Went to Halifax when Boston was evacuated in March, 1776.

SECRETARIES.

1692. Oct. 7. ISAAC ADDINGTON. Appointed by the new charter. He died March 19, 1714-15.

1715. Mch. 26. ADDINGTON DAVENPORT. } Appointed to keep the seals until His PAUL DUDLEY. } Majesty's pleasure was known.

1715. June 8. SAMUEL WOODWARD. Appointed. He arrived at Boston 22d September, 1715, and was sworn in on the 24th.*

1717. June 17. JOSIAH WILLARD. Was appointed to this office, Woodward having resigned. He arrived at Boston December 12, 1717. He died 1st December, 1756.†

1758. March 2. ANDREW OLIVER. Commissioned. He had acted from the time of Willard's death.

1770. Nov. 12. THOMAS FLUCKER. Commissioned to succeed Oliver.

* 1716. May 10. JOSEPH MARION was sworn as Deputy Secretary.
† 1734. April 23. THADDEUS MASON was sworn as Deputy Secretary.

TREASURERS.

Elected annually by the Legislature, and confirmed by the Governor.

1692.	June 9.	.	.	JOHN PHILLIPS.
1693.	June 17.	.	.	JAMES TAILER.
1714.	June 25.	.	.	JEREMIAH ALLEN.*
1736.	July 5.	.	.	WILLIAM FOYE.†
1753.	June 22.	.	.	HARRISON GRAY.‡

* J. ALLEN died after a long illness 6th January, 1741-2.
† FOYE died 21st March, 1759, aged 78.
‡ GRAY held office till the Revolution, and was a refugee.

THE COUNCIL.

In the Charter 1692 the following gentlemen were named of the Council for that year:—

Simon Bradstreet.	Elisha Hutchinson.	Samuel Heyman.
John Richards.	Robert Pike.	Stephen Mason.
Nathaniel Saltonstall.	Jonathan Corwin.	Thomas Hinckley.
Wait Winthrop.	John Joliffe.	William Bradford.
John Phillips.	Adam Winthrop.	John Walley.
James Russell.	Richard Middlecott.	Barnabas Lothrop.
Samuel Sewall.	John Foster.	Job Alcot.
Samuel Appleton.	Peter Sergeant.	Samuel Daniell.
Bartholomew Gedney.	John Lynde.	Silvanus Davis.
John Hathorne.		

[In the following tables those names which did *not* occur on the preceding page have a star affixed. They may, however, in some cases, be found at an earlier date. A distinguishing figure 1 is placed against those serving in each year.]

Council—Continued.

COUNCILLORS.	1693.	1694.	1695.	1696.	1697.
Wait Winthrop, ...	1	1	1	1	1
William Stoughton, . . .	1	1	1	1	1
Thomas Danforth, . .	1	1	1	1	1
John Pynchon, . . .	1	1	1	1	1
James Russell, . . .	1	1	1	1	1
Bartholomew Gedney, . .	1	1	1	1	1
John Hathorne, . . .	1	1	1	1	1
Elisha Hutchinson, . . .	1	1	1	1	1
Isaac Addington, . . .	1	1	1	1	1
Samuel Sewall, . . .	1	1	1	1	1
Daniel Pierce, . . .	1	1	1	1	1
William Browne, . . .	1	1	1	1	1
Nathaniel Thomas, . . .	1	1	1	1	1
John Saflin, . . .	1	1	1	1	1
John Phillips, . . .	1	1	1	1	1
Jonathan Corwin, . . .	1	1	1	1	1
John Foster, . . .	1	1	1	1	1
Peter Sergeant, . . .	1	1	1	1	1
William Bradford, . . .	1	1	1	1	1
Barnabas Lothrop, . . .	1	1	1	1	1
Charles Frost, . . .	1	1	1	1	1
John Walley, . . .	1	–	–	1	1
Nathaniel Saltonstall, . . .	1	1	–	–	–
Robert Pike, . . .	1	1	1	–	–
Francis Hooke, . . .	1	1	–	–	–
John Richards, .. .	1	–	–	–	–
Samuel Donnell, (or Daniell,) .	1	–	–	–	–
Silvanus Davis, . . .	1	–	–	–	–
Elisha Cooke, . . .	–	1	1	1	1
John Thatcher, . .	–	1	1	1	1
Samuel Wheelwright, . .	–	1	1	1	1
Joseph Lynde, . . .	–	1	1	1	1
Samuel Shrimpton, . .	–	–	1	1	1
Eliakim Hutchinson, . .	–	–	1	1	1
	28	28	28	28	28

Council—Continued.

COUNCILLORS.	1698.	1699.	1700.	1701.	1702.
Wait Winthrop, . .	1	1	1	1	1
William Stoughton, .	1	1	1	1	–
Thomas Danforth, .	1	1	–	–	–
John Pynchon, . .	1	1	1	1	1
James Russell, .	1	1	1	1	1
John Hathorne, . .	1	1	1	1	1
Elisha Hutchinson, .	1	1	1	1	1
Isaac Addington, . .	1	1	1	1	1
Samuel Sewall, . . .	1	1	1	1	1
Daniel Peirce, . . .	1	1	1	1	1
William Browne, . .	1	1	1	1	1
Nathaniel Thomas, . .	1	1	1	1	1
John Saffin, ...	1	1	–	–	–
John Phillips, . . .	1	1	1	1	1
Jonathan Corwin, . . .	1	1	1	1	1
John Foster, ...	1	1	1	1	1
Peter Sergeant, . .	1	1	1	1	1
Barnabas Lothrop, . .	1	1	1	1	1
William Bradford, . .	1	–	–	–	–
John Walley, . . .	1	1	1	1	1
Elisha Cooke, . . .	1	1	1	1	1
John Thatcher, . . .	1	1	1	1	1
Joseph Lynde, . . .	1	1	1	1	1
Samuel Wheelwright, . .	1	1	–	–	–
Eliakim Hutchinson, . .	1	1	1	1	1
John Appleton,* . . .	1	1	1	1	1
Penn Townsend,* . . .	1	1	1	1	1
Joseph Hammond,* . .	1	1	1	1	1
Nathaniel Byfield,*, . .	–	1	1	1	1
John Higginson,* . . .	–	–	1	1	1
Samuel Partridge,* . .	–	–	1	1	1
Samuel Donnell, (or Daniell,) .	–	–	1	–	–
Benjamin Browne,* . .	–	–	–	1	1
Andrew Belcher,* . .	–	–	–	–	1
	28	28	28	28	28

Council—Continued.

COUNCILLORS.	1703.	1704.	1705.	1706.	1707.
Wait Winthrop,	1	1	1	1	1
James Russell,	1	1	1	1	1
John Hathorne,	1	1	1	1	1
Elisha Hutchinson,	1	1	1	1	1
Isaac Addington,	1	1	1	1	1
Samuel Sewall,	1	1	1	1	1
Daniel Peirce,	1	–	–	–	–
William Browne,	1	1	1	1	1
John Phillips,	1	1	1	1	1
Jonathan Corwin,	1	1	1	1	1
John Foster,	1	1	1	1	1
John Walley,	1	1	1	1	–
John Thatcher,	1	1	1	1	1
Joseph Lynde,	1	1	1	–	1
Eliakim Hutchinson,	1	1	1	1	1
Penn Townsend,	1	1	1	1	1
Joseph Hammond,	1	–	1	–	–
John Higginson,	1	1	1	1	1
Samuel Partridge,	1	1	1	1	1
Benjamin Brown,	1	1	1	1	1
Andrew Belcher,	1	1	1	1	1
Edward Bromfield,*	1	1	1	1	1
Samuel Hayman,*	1	1	1	–	–
Samuel Legg,*	1	1	1	1	–
Ephraim Hunt,*	1	1	1	1	1
Samuel Appleton,*	1	1	1	1	1
Isaac Winslow,*	1	1	1	1	1
Nathaniel Payne,*	1	1	1	1	1
Nathaniel Byfield,*	–	1	–	–	–
Simeon Stoddard,*	–	1	1	–	1
John Cushing,*	–	–	–	1	–
Ichabod Plaisted,*	–	–	–	1	1
John Leverett,*	–	–	–	1	–
John Appleton,*	–	–	–	1	1
Peter Sergeant,*	–	–	–	–	1
John Cushing, Jr.,*	–	–	–	–	1
	28	28	28	28	28

Council—Continued.

COUNCILLORS.	1708.	1709.	1710.	1711.	1712.	1713.
Wait Winthrop,	1	1	1	1	1	–
James Russell,	1	–	–	–	–	–
John Hathorne,	1	1	1	1	1	–
Elisha Hutchinson,	1	1	1	1	1	1
Isaac Addington,	1	1	1	1	1	1
Samuel Sewall,	1	1	1	1	1	1
William Browne,	1	1	1	1	1	1
John Phillips,	1	1	1	1	1	1
Jonathan Corwin,	1	1	1	1	1	1
John Foster,	1	1	1	–	–	–
Joseph Lynde,	1	1	1	1	1	1
Eliakim Hutchinson,	1	1	1	1	1	1
John Higginson,	1	1	1	1	1	1
Samuel Partridge,	1	1	1	1	1	1
Andrew Belcher,	1	1	1	1	1	1
Edward Bromfield,	1	1	1	1	1	1
Ephraim Hunt,	1	1	1	1	1	1
Samuel Appleton,	1	–	–	–	–	1
Isaac Winslow,	1	1	1	1	1	1
Ichabod Plaisted,	1	1	1	1	1	1
John Appleton,	1	1	1	1	1	1
Peter Sergeant,	1	1	1	1	1	1
John Cushing, Jr.,	1	1	1	1	1	1
Nathaniel Norden,*	1	1	1	1	1	1
John Otis,*.	1	1	1	1	1	1
John Wheelwright,*	1	1	1	1	1	1
Daniel Epes,*	1	1	1	1	1	1
Joseph Church,*.	1	–	–	–	–	–
Nathaniel Payne,*	–	1	1	1	1	1
John Walley,*	–	1	1	1	–	–
Penn Townsend,*	–	1	1	1	1	1
Thomas Noyes,*	–	–	–	1	1	1
William Tailer,*.	–	–	–	–	1	1
Benjamin Lynde,*	–	–	–	–	–	1
	28	28	28	28	28	28

Council—Continued.

COUNCILLORS.	1714.	1715.	1716.
Wait Winthrop, .	1	1	1
Elisha Hutchinson,	1	1	1
Isaac Addington, .	1	-	-
Samuel Sewall, .	1	1	1
John Phillips,	1	-	-
Jonathan Corwin,	1	-	-
Joseph Lynde, .	1	1	1
Eliakim Hutchinson,	1	1	1
John Higginson, .	1	1	1
Samuel Partridge,	1	-	-
Andrew Belcher, .	1	1	1
Edward Bromfield,	1	1	1
Samuel Appleton,	1	-	-
Isaac Winslow, .	1	1	1
Ichabod Plaisted,	1	1	-
John Appleton, .	1	1	1
John Cushing, Jr.,	1	1	1
Nathaniel Norden,	1	1	1
John Otis, .	1	1	1
John Wheelwright,	1	1	1
Nathaniel Payne,	1	1	1
Thomas Noyes, .	1	-	1
William Tailer, .	1	1	1
Benjamin Lynde,	1	1	1
Penn Townsend, .	1	-	1
Addington Davenport,*	1	1	1
Thomas Hutchinson,* .	1	1	1
John Clark,*	1	1	1
Elisha Cooke,*	-	1	-
Samuel Brown,* .	-	1	1
John Pynchon,* .	-	1	1
Thomas Oliver,* .	-	1	-
Thomas Fitch,* .	-	1	1
Edmund Quincy,*	-	1	1
Nathaniel Byfield,*	-	-	1
Adam Winthrop,*	-	1	1
	28	28	28

Council—Continued.

COUNCILLORS.	1717.	1718.	1719.	1720.
Wait Winthrop,	1	–	–	–
Elisha Hutchinson,	1	–	–	–
Samuel Sewall,	1	1	1	1
Eliakim Hutchinson,	1	–	–	–
John Higginson,	1	1	1	–
Andrew Belcher,	1	–	–	–
Edward Bromfield,	1	1	1	1
Isaac Winslow,	1	1	1	1
John Appleton,	1	1	1	1
John Cushing,	1	1	1	1
Nathaniel Norden,	1	1	1	1
John Otis,	1	1	1	1
John Wheelwright,	1	1	1	1
Nathaniel Payne,	1	1	1	1
Thomas Noyes,	1	1	–	–
William Tailer,	1	1	1	1
Benjamin Lynde,	1	1	1	1
Penn Townsend,	1	1	1	1
Addington Davenport,	1	1	1	1
Thomas Hutchinson,	1	1	1	1
John Clark,	1	1	1	–
Elisha Cooke,	1	–	–	–
Samuel Browne,	1	1	1	1
Thomas Fitch,	1	1	1	1
Edmund Quincy,	1	1	1	1
Nathaniel Byfield,	1	1	1	–
Adam Winthrop,	1	1	–	–
William Dummer,*	1	1	1	1
Samuel Partridge,*	–	1	1	1
Jonathan Belcher,*	–	1	1	1
Jonathan Dowse,*	–	1	1	1
Joseph Hammond,*	–	1	1	1
Paul Dudley,*	–	1	1	1
Samuel Thaxter,*	–	–	1	1
Charles Frost,*	–	–	1	1
John Burrill,*	–	–	–	1
	28	28	28	26

Council—Continued.

COUNCILLORS.	1721.	1722.	1723.	1724.
Samuel Sewall, ...	1	1	1	1
Edward Bromfield, ...	1	1	1	1
Isaac Winslow, ...	1	1	1	1
John Appleton, ...	1	1	1	–
John Cushing, ...	1	1	1	1
Nathaniel Norden, ...	1	1	1	–
John Otis, ...	1	1	1	1
John Wheelwright, ...	1	1	1	1
William Tailer, ...	1	1	1	1
Benjamin Lynde, ...	1	1	1	1
Penn Townsend, ...	1	1	1	1
Addington Davenport, ...	1	1	1	1
Thomas Hutchinson, ...	1	1	1	–
Samuel Browne, ...	1	1	1	1
Thomas Fitch, ...	1	1	1	1
Edmund Quincy, ...	1	1	1	1
Adam Winthrop, ...	1	1	1	1
Samuel Partridge, ...	1	1	1	–
Jonathan Dowse, ...	1	1	1	1
Joseph Hammond, ...	1	1	1	1
Thomas Noyes, ...	1	–	–	–
Paul Dudley, ...	1	1	1	1
Samuel Thaxter, ...	1	1	1	1
Charles Frost, ...	1	1	1	1
John Burrill, ...	1	–	–	–
John Turner,*	1	1	1	1
Spencer Phips,*	1	1	1	–
Jonathan Belcher,*	–	1	1	–
William Dummer,*	–	1	–	–
Nathaniel Payne,*	–	1	1	–
Nathaniel Byfield,*	–	–	–	1
Elisha Cooke,*	–	–	–	1
Daniel Oliver,*	–	–	–	1
Symonds Epes,*	–	–	–	1
Thomas Palmer,*	–	–	–	1
Meletiah Bourn,*	–	–	–	1
John Stoddard,*	–	–	–	1
John Clark,*	–	–	–	1
	27	28	27	28

Council—Continued.

COUNCILLORS.	1725.	1726.	1727.	1728.
Samuel Sewall, .	1	–	–	–
Isaac Winslow, .	–	1	1	1
John Cushing, .	1	1	1	1
John Otis, .	1	1	1	–
John Wheelwright, .	1	1	1	1
William Tailer, .	1	1	1	1
Benjamin Lynde, .	1	1	1	1
Penn Townsend, .	1	1	1	–
Addington Davenport, .	1	1	1	1
Thomas Hutchinson, .	1	1	–	1
Samuel Browne, .	1	1	1	1
Thomas Fitch, .	1	1	1	1
Edmund Quincy, .	1	1	1	1
Adam Winthrop, .	1	1	–	1
Jonathan Dowse, .	1	1	–	1
Joseph Hammond, .	1	1	1	1
Paul Dudley, .	1	1	1	1
Samuel Thaxter, .	1	1	1	1
John Turner, .	1	1	1	1
Spencer Phips, .	1	1	1	1
Nathaniel Byfield,, .	1	1	1	1
Elisha Cooke, ..	1	1	–	1
Daniel Oliver, .	1	1	1	1
Symonds Epes, .	1	1	1	1
Thomas Palmer, . .	1	1	–	–
Meletiah Bourn, .	1	1	1	1
John Stoddard, .	–	–	1	1
John Clark, .	1	1	–	–
Edward Hutchinson,* .	1	1	–	–
Jonathan Belcher,* .	–	1	1	–
Jonathan Remington,* .	–	–	1	–
Timothy Lindall,* .	–	–	1	1
John Chandler,* .	–	–	1	1
Charles Chambers,* .	–	–	1	1
Theophilus Burrill,* .	–	–	1	1
William Pepperrell, Jr.,* .	–	–	1	1
	27	28	28	28

Council—Continued.

COUNCILLORS.	1729.	1730.	1731.	1732.
Isaac Winslow,	1	1	1	1
John Wheelwright,	1	1	1	1
William Tailer,	1	–	–	–
Benjamin Lynde,	1	1	1	1
Addington Davenport, *	1	–	–	–
Thomas Hutchinson,	1	1	1	1
Samuel Browne,	1	1	–	–
Thomas Fitch,	1	1	–	–
Edmund Quincy,	1	–	–	–
Adam Winthrop,	1	–	–	–
Jonathan Dowse,	1	1	1	–
Paul Dudley,	1	–	1	1
Samuel Thaxter,	1	1	1	1
John Turner,	1	1	1	1
Spencer Phips,	1	1	1	1
Daniel Oliver,	1	1	1	1
Symonds Epes,	1	1	1	1
Thomas Palmer,	–	1	1	1
Meletiah Bourne,	1	1	1	–
Timothy Lindall,	1	1	–	–
John Chandler,	1	1	1	1
Charles Chambers,	1	1	–	–
Theophilus Burrill,	1	1	–	–
William Pepperrell, Jr.,	1	1	1	1
Joseph Hammond,	1	–	–	–
William Dudley,*	1	1	1	1
Peter Thatcher,*	1	1	1	–
Jonathan Remington,*	–	1	1	1
William Clarke,*	–	1	1	1
John Alford,*	–	1	1	1
Seth Williams,*	–	1	1	1
Timothy Gerrish,*	–	1	1	1
Ebenezer Stone,*	–	1	1	1
Nathaniel Coffin,*	–	1	–	–
Thomas Cushing,*	–	–	1	1
Joseph Wadsworth,*	–	–	1	1
John Osborne,*	–	–	1	1
Ebenezer Burrill,*	–	–	1	1
Ezekiel Lewis,*	–	–	1	1
Isaac Lothrop,*	–	–	–	1
Francis Foxcroft,*	–	–	–	1
	26	28	28	27

Council—Continued.

COUNCILLORS.	1733.	1734.	1735.	1736.
Isaac Winslow, .	1	1	1	1
Benjamin Lynde, .	1	1	1	1
Thomas Hutchinson, .	1	1	1	1
Addington Davenport,	–	1	–	–
Thomas Fitch, .	–	1	–	–
Edmund Quincy,	–	1	1	1
Paul Dudley, .	1	1	1	1
Samuel Thaxter, .	1	1	1	1
John Turner, .	1	1	1	1
Symonds Epes, .	1	1	–	–
Thomas Palmer, .	1	–	–	–
Meletiah Bourne,	1	1	1	1
William Pepperrell, Jr.,	1	1	1	1
William Dudley,	1	1	1	1
Jonathan Remington, .	1	1	1	1
William Clarke, .	1	–	–	–
John Alford,	1	–	–	–
Seth Williams, .	1	1	1	1
Timothy Gerrish,	1	1	–	–
Ebenezer Stone, .	1	–	–	–
Thomas Cushing,	1	1	1	1
Joseph Wadsworth,	1	–	–	–
John Osborne, .	1	1	1	1
Ebenezer Burrill,	1	1	1	1
Ezekiel Lewis, .	1	1	1	–
Isaac Lothrop, .	1	1	1	1
Francis Foxcroft,	1	1	1	1
Samuel Came,* .	1	1	1	1
John Jeffries,* .	1 *	1	1	1
Edward Goddard,*	1	1	1	–
Josiah Willard,* .	–	1	1	1
Jacob Wendell,*	–	1	1	1
Samuel Welles,*	–	1	1	1
Anthony Stoddard,* .	–	–	1	1
Jeremiah Moulton,*	–	–	1	1
Thomas Berry,* .	–	–	1	1
Joseph Wilder,* .	–	–	1	1
Ebenezer Pomeroy,*	–	–	–	1
John Cushing,* .	–	–	–	1
	27	28	28	28

Council—Continued.

COUNCILLORS.	1737.	1738.	1739.	1740.	1741.
Thomas Hutchinson, . . .	1	1	1	–	–
Edmund Quincy, ...	1	–	–	–	–
Samuel Thatcher, . . .	1	–	–	–	–
John Turner, ...	1	1	1	1	–
Meletiah Bourne, ...	1	1	1	–	–
William Pepperrell, . . .	1	1	1	1	1
William Dudley, ...	1	1	1	1	–
Jonathan Remington, . . .	1	1	1	1	–
Seth Williams, ...	1	1	1	–	–
John Osborne, ...	1	1	1	1	–
Ebenezer Burrill, ...	1	1	1	1	–
Francis Foxcroft, ...	1	1	1	1	1
Samuel Cane, ...	1	1	1	1	1
John Jeffries, ...	1	1	1	1	1
Josiah Willard, ...	1	1	1	1	1
Jacob Wendell, ...	1	1	1	1	1
Samuel Welles, ...	1	1	–	1	–
Anthony Stoddard, . . .	1	1	1	1	1
Jeremiah Moulton, . . .	1	1	1	1	1
Thomas Berry, ...	1	1	1	1	–
Joseph Wilder, ...	1	1	1	1	–
John Cushing, ...	1	1	1	1	1
John Stoddard,*	1	1	–	–	–
Benjamin Lynde, Jr.,* . . .	1	1	1	1	–
Nathaniel Hubbard,* . . .	1	1	1	1	–
Richard Bill,*	1	1	1	1	1
Daniel Russell,*	1	1	1	1	–
William Dummer,* . . .	–	1	1	–	–
Ezekiel Lewis,*	–	1	1	1	–
Edward Hutchinson,* . . .	–	1	1	1	–
Samuel Danforth,* . . .	–	–	1	1	1
Shubal Gorham,*	–	–	–	1	1
William Brown,*	–	–	–	1	–
William Foye,*	–	–	–	–	1
John Reed,*	–	–	–	–	1
John Greenleaf,*	–	–	–	–	1
	27	28	27	26	15

Council—Continued.

COUNCILLORS.	1742.	1743.	1744.	1745.
William Pepperrell, ...	1	1	1	1
Francis Foxcroft, ...	1	1	1	1
William Dudley, ...	1	1	–	–
John Osborne, ...	1	1	1	1
Ebenezer Burrill, ...	1	1	–	–
John Jeffries, ...	1	1	1	–
Josiah Willard, ...	1	1	1	1
Jacob Wendell, ...	1	1	1	1
Anthony Stoddard, ...	1	–	–	–
Jeremiah Moulton, ...	1	1	1	1
Joseph Wilder, ...	1	1	1	1
John Cushing, ...	1	1	1	1
Benjamin Lynde, Jr., ...	–	1	1	1
Daniel Russell, ...	1	–	1	1
Ezekiel Lewis, ...	1	–	–	–
Samuel Danforth, ...	1	1	1	1
Shubal Gorham, ...	1	1	–	–
William Browne, ...	–	–	1	1
William Foye, ...	1	1	1	1
John Reed, ...	1	–	–	–
John Greenleaf, ...	1	1	1	1
Thomas Berry,*	1	1	1	1
Samuel Waldo,*	1	1	1	1
Samuel Watts,*	1	1	1	1
Nathaniel Hubbard,*	1	1	1	1
George Leonard,*	1	1	1	1
John Hill,*	1	1	1	1
James Allen,*	1	–	–	–
Joseph Dwight,*	1	1	1	1
John Quincy,*	1	–	–	–
Richard Saltonstall,*	–	1	1	1
John Chandler,*	–	1	1	1
Ezekiel Cheever,*	–	1	1	1
Sylvanus Bourne,*	–	1	1	1
Isaac Little,*	–	1	–	–
Eliakim Hutchinson,*	–	–	1	1
James Bowdoin,*	–	–	1	1
John Wheelwright,*	–	–	–	1
	28	28	28	28

Council—Continued.

COUNCILLORS.	1746.	1747.	1748.	1749.	1750.	1751.
Sir William Pepperrell, .	1	1	1	1	1	1
Francis Foxcroft, .	1	1	1	1	1	1
John Osborne,	1	1	1	1	1	1
Josiah Willard,	1	1	1	1	1	1
Jacob Wendell,	1	1	1	1	1	1
Jeremiah Moulton,	1	1	1	1	1	1
Joseph Wilder, .	1	1	1	1	1	1
John Cushing, .	1	1	1	1	1	1
Benjamin Lynde, . .	1	1	1	·1	1	1
Daniel Russell, .	1	1	1	1	1	1
Ezekiel Lewis, .	–	1	1	1	1	1
Samuel Danforth, . .	1	1	1	1	1	1
William Foye, .	1	1	1	1	1	1
John Greenleaf, .	1	1	1	1	1	1
Thomas Berry, .	1	1	1	1	1	–
Samuel Watts, .	1	1	1	1	1	1
George Leonard, .	1	1	1	1	1	1
John Hill, . .	1	1	1	1	1	1
Joseph Dwight,	1	–	–	–	–	–
John Chandler, .	1	1	1	1	1	1
Ezekiel Cheever, . .	1	1	1	1	1	1
Sylvanus Bourne, . .	1	1	1	1	1	1
Eliakim Hutchinson,	1	–	–	–	–	–
James Bowdoin, .	1	–	–	–	–	–
John Wheelwright,	1	1	1	1	1	1
Ebenezer Burrill, .	1	–	–	–	–	–
James Minot,* .	1	1	1	1	1	1
Andrew Oliver,* .	1	1	1	1	1	1
Perez Bradford,* .	1	–	–	–	–	–
Samuel Welles,* .	–	1	1	–	–	–
John Quincy,* .	–	1	1	1	1	1
Joseph Pynchon,* .	–	1	1	1	1	1
John Otis,* . .	–	1	1	1	1	1
Thomas Hutchinson,* .	–	–	–	1	1	1
	28	28	28	28	28	27

Council—Continued.

COUNCILLORS.			1752.	1753.	1754.	1755.	1756.
Sir William Pepperrell,	.	.	1	1	1	1	1
Francis Foxcroft,	.	.	1	1	1	1	1
John Osborne,	.	.	1	1	1	1	1
Josiah Willard,	.	.	1	1	1	1	—
Jacob Wendell,	.	.	1	1	1	1	1
Joseph Wilder,	.	.	1	—	—	—	—
John Cushing,	.	.	1	1	1	1	1
Benjamin Lynde,	.	.	1	1	1	1	1
Daniel Russell,	.	.	1	1	1	1	1
Ezekiel Lewis,	.	.	1	—	—	—	—
Samuel Danforth,	.	.	1	1	1	1	1
John Greenleaf,	.	.	1	1	1	1	1
Samuel Watts,	.	.	1	1	1	1	1
George Leonard,	.	.	1	1	1	1	1
John Hill,	.	.	1	1	1	1	1
John Chandler,	.	.	1	1	1	1	1
Ezekiel Cheever,	.	.	1	1	1	1	1
Sylvanus Bourne,	.	.	1	1	1	1	1
John Wheelwright,	.	.	1	1	1	—	—
James Minot,	.	.	1	1	1	1	1
Andrew Oliver,	.	.	1	1	1	1	1
John Otis,	.	.	1	1	1	1	1
Joseph Pynchon,	.	.	1	1	1	1	1
Thomas Hutchinson,	.	.	1	1	1	1	1
John Quincy,	.	.	1	1	—	—	—
Stephen Sewall,*	.	.	1	1	1	1	1
Jabez Fox,*	.	.	1	1	1	—	—
Isaac Royall,*	.	.	1	1	1	1	1
Eleazer Porter,*	.	.	—	1	1	1	1
Benjamin Lincoln,*	.	.	—	1	1	1	1
John Erving,*	.	.	—	—	1	1	1
Richard Cutt,*	.	.	—	—	—	1	1
William Brattle,*	.	.	—	—	—	1	1
Benjamin Pickman,*	.	.	—	—	—	—	1
			28	28	28	28	28

Council—Continued.

COUNCILLORS.	1757.	1758.	1759.	1760.
Sir William Pepperrell,	1	1	1	–
Francis Foxcroft,	1	–	–	–
John Osborne,	1	1	1	1
Jacob Wendell,	1	1	1	1
John Cushing,	1	1	1	1
Benjamin Lynde,	1	1	1	1
Samuel Danforth,	1	1	1	1
Samuel Watts,	1	1	1	1
George Leonard,	1	1	1	1
John Hill,	1	1	1	1
John Chandler,	1	1	1	1
Ezekiel Cheever,	1	1	1	1
Sylvanus Bourne,	1	1	1	1
James Minot,	1	1	–	–
Andrew Oliver,	1	1	1	1
Joseph Pynchon,	1	1	1	–
Thomas Hutchinson,	1	1	1	1
Stephen Sewall,	1	1	1	1
Isaac Royall,	1	1	1	1
Eleazer Porter,	1	–	–	–
Richard Cutt,	1	1	1	1
William Brattle,	1	1	1	1
Benjamin Pickman,	1	1	–	–
John Erving,	1	1	1	1
Benjamin Lincoln,	1	1	1	1
Robert Hooper,*.	1	1	–	–
James Bowdoin,*	1	1	1	1
Gamaliel Bradford,*	1	1	1	1
Thomas Hancock,*	–	1	1	1
Samuel Waldo,*	–	1	–	–
Thomas Hubbard,*	–	–	1	1
Ichabod Plaisted,*	–	–	1	1
Chambers Russell,*	–	–	1	1
Peter Oliver,*	–	–	1	1
Israel Williams,*	–	–	–	1
Nathaniel Sparhawk,*	–	–	–	1
	28	28	28	28

COUNCILLORS.	1761.	1762.	1763.	1764.
John Osborne,	1	1	1	—
John Cushing,	1	1	1	—
Benjamin Lynde,	1	1	1	1
Samuel Danforth,	1	1	1	1
Samuel Watts,	1	1	1	—
George Leonard,	1	1	1	1
John Hill,	1	1	1	1
John Chandler,	1	1	—	—
Sylvanus Bourne,	1	—	—	—
Andrew Oliver,	1	1	1	1
Thomas Hutchinson,	1	1	1	1
Isaac Royall,	1	1	1	1
Richard Cutt,	1	1	—	—
William Brattle,	1	1	1	1
John Erving,	1	1	1	1
Benjamin Lincoln,	1	1	1	1
James Bowdoin,	1	1	1	1
Gamaliel Bradford,	1	1	1	1
Thomas Hancock,	1	1	1	1
Thomas Hubbard,	1	1	1	1
Ichabod Plaisted,	1	—	—	—
Peter Oliver,	1	1	1	1
Israel Williams,	1	1	1	1
Nathaniel Sparhawk,	1	1	1	1
Harrison Gray,*	1	1	1	1
John Choate,*	1	1	1	1
James Russell,*	1	1	1	1
Thomas Flucker,*	1	1	1	1
Nathaniel Ropes,*	—	1	1	1
James Otis,*	—	1	1	1
Timothy Paine,*	—	—	1	1
John Bradbury,*	—	—	1	1
Timothy Ruggles,*	—	—	—	1
Royall Tyler,*	—	—	—	1
Edmund Trowbridge,*	—	—	—	1
	28	28	28	28

Council—Continued.

' COUNCILLORS.	1765.	1766.	1767.	1768.	1769.
Benjamin Lynde,	1	–	–	–	–
Samuel Danforth,	1	1	1	1	1
George Leonard,	1	–	–	–	–
John Hill,	1	1	1	1	1
Andrew Oliver,	1	–	–	–	–
Thomas Hutchinson,	1	–	–	–	–
Isaac Royall,	1	1	1	1	1
William Brattle,	1	1	1	1	–
John Erving,	1	1	1	1	1
Benjamin Lincoln,	1	1	1	1	1
James Bowdoin,	1	1	1	1	–
Gamaliel Bradford,	1	1	1	1	1
Thomas Hubbard,	1	1	1	1	1
Peter Oliver,	1	–	–	–	–
Israel Williams,	1	1	–	–	–
Nathaniel Sparhawk,	1	–	1	1	1
Harrison Gray,	1	1	1	1	1
John Choate,	1	–	–	–	–
James Russell,	1	1	1	1	1
Thomas Flucker,	1	1	1	1	–
Nathaniel Ropes,	1	1	1	1	
James Otis,	1	–	–	–	–
Timothy Paine,	1	1	1	1	–
John Bradbury,	1	1	1	1	1
Royall Tyler,	1	1	1	1	1
Edmund Trowbridge,	1	–	–	–	–
Andrew Belcher,*	1	1	1	–	–
John Chandler,*	1	1	1	–	–
Samuel White,*	–	1	1	1	–
Jeremiah Powell,*	–	1	1	1	1
John Worthington,*	–	–	1	1	–
Samuel Dexter,*	–	–	–	1	1
William Sever,*	–	–	–	–	1
James Pitts,*	–	1	1	1	1
	28	22	23	22	16

Council—Continued.

COUNCILLORS.	1770.	1771.	1772.	1773.	1774.
Samuel Danforth, . .	1	1	1	1	1
Isaac Royall, . .	1	1	1	1	–
William Brattle, . . .	1	1	1	1	–
John Erving, ...	1	1	1	1	1
James Bowdoin, ...	1	1	1	1	–
Thomas Hubbard, . .	1	1	1	–	–
Nathaniel Sparhawk, . .	1	1	1	–	–
Harrison Gray, . . .	1	1	1	–	–
James Russell, . . .	1	1	1	1	–
James Otis, . . .	1	1	1	1	1
John Bradbury, . . .	1	1	1	–	–
Royall Tyler, . . .	1	–	–	–	–
James Fitts, . . .	1	1	1	1	1
Jeremiah Powell, . . .	1	1	1	–	1
Samuel Dexter, . . .	1	1	1	1	–
William Sever, . . .	1	1	1	1	1
Benjamin Greenleaf,* . .	1	1	1	1	1
Thomas Saunders, Jr.,* .	1	1	1	–	–
Joseph Gerrish,* . . .	1	–	–	–	–
Joshua Henshaw,* . .	1	1	–	–	–
Artemas Ward,* . . .	1	1	1	1	1
Stephen Hall,* . . .	1	1	1	–	–
Walter Spooner,* . . .	1	1	1	1	1
James Gowen,* . . .	1	1	1	1	–
George Leonard, Jr.,* . .	1	1	1	1	1
James Humphrey,* . .	1	1	1	1	–
Caleb Cushing,* . . .	–	1	1	1	1
Timothy Woodbridge,* .	–	1	1	1	–
John Hancock,* . . .	–	–	1	1	–
Samuel Phillips,* . .	–	–	1	1	1
Humphrey Hobson,* . .	–	–	–	1	–
John Winthrop,* . .	–	–	–	1	–
John Whitcomb,* . .	–	–	–	1	–
Jedidiah Preble,* . .	–	–	–	1	1
Richard Derby, Jr.,* .	–	–	–	–	1
Benjamin Chadbourn,* .	–	–	–	–	1
	26	26	27	24	15

MANDAMUS COUNCILLORS.

The following were appointed by His Majesty Councillors of this Province, by Writ of Mandamus, 9 Aug. 1774.

The first ten, marked with a star, alone took the oath of office.

Thomas Flucker.*	Thomas Hutchinson, Jr.	Josiah Edson.
Foster Hutchinson.*	Samuel Danforth.	Richard Lechmere.
Harrison Gray.* —	John Erving, Jr.	John Worthington.
Joseph Lee.*	James Russell.	Timothy Paine.
Isaac Winslow.*	Timothy Ruggles.	Jeremiah Powell.
William Browne.*	Israel Williams.	Jonathan Simpson.
James Boutineau.*	George Watson.	John Murray.
Joshua Loring.*	Nathaniel Ray Thomas.	Daniel Leonard.
William Pepperrell.*	Timothy Woodbridge.	Thomas Palmer.
John Erving, Jr.*	William Vassall.	Isaac Royall.
Thomas Oliver.	Joseph Greene.	Robert Hooper.
Peter Oliver.	Andrew Oliver.	Abijah Willard.

NOTES.

1693. Elisha Cooke was elected and negatived.

1701. Jonathan Corwin was negatived, but, June 3rd, was accepted by the Governor.

1703. Elisha Cooke, Peter Sergeant, Thomas Oakes, John Saffin and John Bradford were negatived.

1703. May 26. A message was sent up from the House in the words following: "That this House are of Opinion that every Person who is chosen a Councellour for this Province ought to have the Voice of the Major Part of the Electors, and therefore Moved that the Election of Councellours be so made at this Time and for the Future, which they apprehend most agreeable to the Charter."
"His Excellency signified his Dissent therefrom in the following Words, viz.: 'I do not Consent to this Vote, the Charter directing the choice of twenty-eight Councellours for her Majesties service, which may fail by this Method, and it being contrary to the usage of the General assembly in any election past since the Granting of the present Charter of this Province': and directed that the elections be made after the former manner and usage."
After the election "His Excellency sent a message saying 'that there were several gentlemen left out that were of the Council last year, who were of good ability for estate and otherwise to serve her Majesty, and well disposed thereto; and that some others who were anew elected were not so well disposed, some of them being of little or mean estate: and withal signified that he should expunge five of the names on their list, viz.: Elisha Cooke, Peter Sargeant, esqs., Mr. Thomas Oakes, Mr. John Saffin, and Mr. Bradford."

1704. Elisha Cooke and Peter Sergeant were negatived, and June 13th Simeon Stoddard and Samuel Hayman were chosen.

1706. Elisha Cooke and Joseph Hammond were negatived, and June 6th Benjamin Brown and Ephraim Hunt were chosen.

1708. Elisha Cooke and Nathaniel Paine were negatived, and June 23rd Daniel Epes and Joseph Church were chosen.

1714. Nathaniel Byfield was negatived, and June 3rd John Clark was chosen.

1715. Nathaniel Byfield was negatived and no else then chosen. Dec. 3rd four were elected to fill vacancies, viz.: Penn Townsend, Nathaniel Byfield, Thomas Noyes and Adam Winthrop.

1718. Elisha Cooke was negatived. He being however a member for the preceding year, "His Excellency having signified to Elisha Cooke, esq., that he excused his attendance at the Board as one of his Majesties Council for the present year, he withdrew." May 30th Paul Dudley was chosen.

1720. Nathaniel Byfield and John Clark were negatived.

1721. **Nathaniel Byfield** was negatived.

1722. **Nathaniel Byfield** and William Clark were negatived, and June 29th Nathaniel Payne and William Dummer were chosen.

1723. **Nathaniel** Byfield was negatived.

1725. William Throop was negatived.

1729. Jonathan Belcher and Isaac Little were negatived.

1732. Isaac Little was negatived.

1733. Payne Mayhew was negatived.

1737. Paul Dudley was negatived.

1739. Paul Dudley was negatived.

1740. Paul Dudley and Isaac Little were negatived.

1741. Thirteen were negatived, viz.: Edward Goddard, Daniel Epes, James Minot, Samuel White, Samuel Adams, William Stoddard, Estes Hatch, Thomas Norton, Ephraim Wilder, Henry Burchstead, Dr. John Clark, George Leonard, John Otis.

The Governor then dissolved the House, sending the following Message: "The management of the elections made yesterday discover to me so much of the inclination of your House to support the fraudulent pernicious scheme commonly called the Land Bank, condemned at home by His Majesty and both Houses of Parliament of Great Britain, that I judge it derogatory to the King's honour and service and inconsistent with the peace and welfare of this people, that you sit any longer in General Assembly; and I have therefore directed Mr. Secretary to declare this Court dissolved."

The vacancies in the Council seem to have remained unfilled all the year.

1751. Isaac Royall was negatived as his "choice appears to be attended with such circumstances in relation to his own conduct in that affair, as may (if countenanced) be of evil influence and example in future elections."

1766. Joseph Gerrish, Thomas Saunders, James Otis, Jerathmeel Bowers, Nathaniel Sparhawk and Samuel Dexter were negatived. Six in all.

1767. Joseph Gerrish, Thomas Saunders, James Otis, Jerathmeel Bowers and Samuel Dexter were negatived. Five vacancies.

1768. Joseph Gerrish, Thomas Saunders, James Otis, Jerathmeel Bowers, John Hancock and Artemas Ward were negatived, making six vacancies.

1769. Eleven were negatived, viz.: William Brattle, Benjamin Greenleaf, James Bowdoin, Artemas Ward, Thomas Saunders, Joseph Gerrish, John Hancock, Joshua Henshaw, James Otis, Jerathmeel Bowers, Walter Spooner.

Joseph Hawley was elected and declined, making twelve vacancies.

1770. John Hancock and Jerathmeel Bowers were negatived.

1771. John Hancock and Jerathmeel Bowers were negatived.

1772. Jerathmeel Bowers was negatived.

1773. Jerathmeel Bowers, William Phillips and John Adams were negatived. Bowers seems to have had a double vote, so that there were four vacancies.

1774. Thirteen were negatived, viz.: James Bowdoin, Samuel Dexter, John Winthrop, Timothy Danielson, Benjamin Austin, William Phillips, Michael Farley, James Prescott, John Adams, Norton Quincy, Jerathmeel Bowers, Enoch Freeman, Jedidiah Foster.

1774. June 17th. Governor Gage dissolved the House.

SPEAKERS OF THE HOUSE OF REPRESENTATIVES.

Date.	Name.	Date.	Name.
1691–2. Mch. 8.	William Bond.	1721. May 31.	John Clark.
1693. May 31.	William Bond.	1722. May 30.	John Clark.
1694. May 30.	Nehemiah Jewett.	1723. May 29.	John Clark.
1695. May 29.	William Bond.	1724. May 27.	William Dudley.
1696. May 27.	Penn Townsend.	1725. May 26.	William Dudley.
1697. May 26.	Penn Townsend.	1726. May 25.	William Dudley.
1698. May 25.	Nathaniel Byfield.	1727. May 31.	William Dudley.
1699. May 31.	James Converse.	1728. May 29.	William Dudley.
1700. May 29.	John Leverett.	1729. May 28.	John Quincy.
1701. May 28.	Nehemiah Jewett.	1730. May 27.	John Quincy.
1702. May 27.	James Converse.	1731. May 26.	John Quincy.
1703. May 26.	James Converse.	1732. May 31.	John Quincy.
1704. May 31.	James Converse.	1733. May 30.	John Quincy.
1705. May 30.	Thomas Oakes.	1734. May 29.	John Quincy.
1706. May 29.	Thomas Oakes.	1735. May 28.	John Quincy.
1707. May 28.	John Burrill.	1736. May 26.	John Quincy.
1708. May 26.	Thomas Oliver.	1737. May 25.	John Quincy.
1709. May 25.	John Clark.	1738. May 31.	John Quincy.
1710. May 31.	John Clark.	1739. May 30.	John Quincy.
1711. May 30.	John Burrill.	1740. May 28.	John Quincy.
1712. May 29.	John Burrill.	1741. { May 27.	William Fairfield.
1713. May 27.	John Burrill.	1741. { July 8.	John Hobson.
1714. May 26.	John Burrill.	1742. May 26.	Thomas Cushing.
1715. May 25.	John Burrill.	1743. May 25.	Thomas Cushing.
1716. May 30.	John Burrill.	1744. May 30.	Thomas Cushing.
1717. May 29.	John Burrill.	1745. May 29.	Thomas Cushing.
1718. May 28.	John Burrill.	1746. May 28.	Thomas Hutchinson.
1719. May 27.	John Burrill.	1747. May 27.	Thomas Hutchinson.
1720. { May 25.	Elisha Cooke.	1748. May 25.	Thomas Hutchinson.
1720. { July 13.	Timothy Lindall.	1749. May 31.	Joseph Dwight.

Speakers of the House of Representatives—Concluded.

DATE.		NAME.	DATE.		NAME.
1750.	May 30.	Thomas Hubbard.	1763.	May 25.	Timothy Ruggles.
1751.	May 29.	Thomas Hubbard.	1764.	May 30.	Samuel White.
1752.	May 27.	Thomas Hubbard.	1765.	May 29.	Samuel White.
1753.	May 30.	Thomas Hubbard.	1766.	May 28.	Thomas Cushing.
1754.	May 29.	Thomas Hubbard.	1767.	May 27.	Thomas Cushing.
1755.	May 28.	Thomas Hubbard.	1768.	May 25.	Thomas Cushing.
1756.	May 26.	Thomas Hubbard.	1769.	May 31.	Thomas Cushing.
1757.	May 25.	Thomas Hubbard.	1770.	May 30.	Thomas Cushing.
1758.	May 31.	Thomas Hubbard.	1771.	May 29.	Thomas Cushing.
1759.	May 30.	Samuel White.	1772.	May 27.	Thomas Cushing.
1760.	May 28.	James Otis.	1773.	May 26.	Thomas Cushing.
1761.	May 27.	James Otis.	1774.	May 25.	Thomas Cushing.
1762.	May 26.	Timothy Ruggles.			

NOTES.

1705. The Governor negatived Oakes, but the House insisted and carried the point.

1720. The Governor negatived Cooke, and as the House would not elect another he dissolved it; the new Court chose Lindall.

1739. Paul Dudley was elected and negatived. The House at once chose Quincy.

1741. Samuel Watts was chosen and negatived, when Fairfield was elected. At the second Court, Hobson was chosen.

1766. James Otis was elected and negatived, and Cushing was then chosen.

SUPERIOR COURT OF JUDICATURE.

DATE OF APPOINTMENT.	NAME OF JUSTICE.

1692.   Dec. 7.   William Stoughton, *Chief Justice*, Thomas Danforth, John Richards, Wait Winthrop, Samuel Sewall, appointed.

Stoughton, Danforth, Richards, Winthrop, Sewall.

1694–5. Mar. 6.   Elisha Cooke, appointed.[1]

Stoughton, Danforth, Winthrop, Sewall, Cooke.

1696.   Oct. 16.   The same confirmed.

1699.   July 17.   The same confirmed.

1700.   June 7.   John Walley, appointed.[2]

Stoughton, Winthrop, Sewall, Cooke, Walley.

1701.   Aug. 1.   John Saffin, appointed.[3]

Winthrop, Sewall, Cooke, Walley, Saffin.

1702.   June 29.   Isaac Addington, *Chief Justice*, Samuel Sewall, John Walley, appointed.[4]

        July 8.   John Leverett, appointed.

        Aug. 14.   John Hathorne, appointed.

Addington, Sewall, Walley, Leverett, Hathorne.

1703.   July 23.   (Addington desires to resign.)[5]

1707–8. Feb. 19.   Wait Winthrop, appointed.[6]

        Feb. 20.   Jonathan Corwin, appointed.[6]

Winthrop, Sewall, Walley, Hathorne, Corwin.

1712.   June 4.   Nathaniel Thomas, appointed.[7]

        June 5.   Benjamin Lynde, appointed.[7]

Winthrop, Sewall, Corwin, Thomas, Lynde.

---

[1] Cooke succeeded John Richards, who died April 4, 1694.

[2] Walley succeeded Thomas Danforth, who died Nov. 5, 1699.

[3] William Stoughton having died July 7, 1701, Winthrop was made C. J., and Saffin added.

[4] Nathaniel Thomas and Nathaniel Byfield were both nominated with the others elected June 29, 1702, but the Council "consented not to the above two."

[5] July 23, 1703. "Isaac Addington, Esq., represented to the Board the decay of his health and incapacity of sustaining the Office of Chief Justice of Her Majesty's Superiour Court of Judicature, and offered his Commission for that place. His Excellency declared that no farther service was expected from him therein at present, and that he would consider with the Council to fill that place as soon as possible."

[6] Feb. 19, 1707–8. Winthrop was appointed Chief Justice in place of Addington. For Associate, Elisha Hutchinson was nominated, but the Council adjourned till the next day, when he declined "being further named for that service," and Corwin was appointed. Leverett had undoubtedly resigned on being appointed President of Harvard College.

[7] There were two vacancies, owing to the death of John Walley, Jan. 11, 1711–12, and the resignation of John Hathorne, "by reason of his great hardness of hearing." Nathaniel Thomas was elected June 4, as

Superior Court of Judicature—Continued.

DATE OF APPOINTMENT	NAME OF JUSTICE.
1715. Dec. 19.	Addington Davenport appointed.[8]
	Winthrop, Sewall, Thomas, Lynde, Davenport.
1718. Apr. 16.	Edmund Quincy, Paul Dudley appointed.[9]
	Sewall, Lynde, Davenport, Quincy, Dudley.
1728. Dec. 12.	Benjamin Lynde, *Chief Justice,* Addington Davenport, Paul Dudley, Edmund Quincy, John Cushing appointed.[10]
	Lynde, Davenport, Dudley, Quincy, Cushing.
1733. June 21.	Benjamin Lynde, Addington Davenport, Paul Dudley, Edmund Quincy, Jonathan Remington appointed.[11]
	Lynde, Davenport, Dudley, Quincy, Remington.
1736. June 22.	(John Stoddard appointed, but did not serve.)[12]
Dec. 29.	Richard Saltonstall appointed.[12]
	Lynde, Dudley, Quincy, Remington, Saltonstall.
1737–8. Jan. 13.	Thomas Greaves appointed.[13]
	Lynde, Dudley, Remington, Saltonstall, Greaves.
1739. May 16.	Stephen Sewall appointed.[14]
	Lynde, Dudley, Remington, Saltonstall, Sewall.
1745–6. Jan. 24.	Paul Dudley, Richard Saltonstall, Stephen Sewall, Nathaniel Hubbard, Benjamin Lynde, (jr.) appointed.[15]
	Dudley, Saltonstall, Sewall, Hubbard, Lynde.
1747–8. Feb. 16.	John Cushing appointed.[16]
	Dudley, Saltonstall, Sewall, Lynde, Cushing.

was also Thomas Brattle, but on the 5th, Brattle desired the Secretary " to return his thanks to the Governor and Council for their respect shown him, and withall to acquaint them that his bodily infirmities and unacquaintedness with the Law, will not allow of his acceptance of the office of a Justice of the Superior Court." Benjamin Lynde was accordingly appointed.

[8] Of the old Board four were re-appointed, Corwin being omitted probably on account of his great age.

[9] There were two vacancies, Wait Winthrop having died Nov. 5, 1717, and Nathaniel Thomas 22 Oct., 1718, aged 75. Sewall was made Chief Justice. Dudley was appointed Nov. 20.

[10] Cushing succeeded Sewall, who resigned on account of age.

[11] Remington succeeded Cushing, who was probably left out on account of his age, as he was 75 years old at his death in 1737.

[12] Addington Davenport died in April, 1736, and John Stoddard was appointed but never served. The vacancy was filled by the selection of Richard Saltonstall.

[13] Thomas Greaves was appointed " in the room of Edmund Quincy, Esq. during the time of his absence abroad in the service of the Province." Greaves received a full appointment Aug. 19, 1738, but resigned the position soon.

[14] Stephen Sewall, "in the room of Thomas Greaves, Esq. resigned."

[15] Benjamin Lynde, Sr., had died Jan. 28, 1744-5, and Jonathan Remington had died Sep. 29, 1745. These vacancies were filled by the appointment of Hubbard and Lynde, the latter being the son of the late Chief Justice. The Council record has Mitchell Sewall for Stephen, a clerical error.

[16] John Cushing, son of the former Judge, took the place of Hubbard, who died probably in that year.

Superior Court of Judicature—Concluded.

DATE OF APPOINTMENT.	NAME OF JUSTICE.
1752. April 4.	Chambers Russell appointed.[17]
	Sewall, Saltonstall, Lynde, Cushing, Russell.
1756. Sept. 14.	Peter Oliver appointed.[18]
	Sewall, Lynde, Cushing, Russell, Oliver.
1760. Nov. 13.	Thomas Hutchinson appointed.[19]
	Hutchinson, Lynde, Cushing, Russell, Oliver.
1761. Apr. 15.	The same five confirmed.
1767. Mch. 25.	Edmund Trowbridge appointed.[20]
	Hutchinson, Lynde, Cushing, Oliver, Trowbridge.
1771. Mch. 21.	Foster Hutchinson appointed.[21]
	Lynde, Cushing, Oliver, Trowbridge, F. Hutchinson.
1772. Jan. 15.	Nathaniel Ropes, William Cushing appointed.[22]
	Oliver, Trowbridge, F. Hutchinson, Ropes, W. Cushing.
1774. June 15.	William Browne appointed.[23]
	Oliver, Trowbridge, F. Hutchinson, W. Cushing, Browne.

[17] Sewall succeeded as Chief after the death of Paul Dudley, Jan. 21, 1751-2, and Russell filled the vacancy.

[18] Oliver was appointed, "Richard Saltonstall having resigned."

[19] Hutchinson was made Chief in the place of Sewall, who died Nov., 1760.

[20] Trowbridge succeeded Russell, who died in England, 24 Nov., 1766.

[21] Foster Hutchinson was appointed, as his brother had become Governor, and Lynde was made C. J.

[22] Ropes and Cushing in place of J. Cushing, who resigned in 1771, as did C. J. Lynde. Oliver became Chief Justice. On March 18th, all but Oliver were again named; perhaps the two old commissions needed renewal.

[23] Browne succeeded Ropes, who died 18 Mch., 1774.

SPECIAL JUSTICES OF THE SUPERIOR COURT.

[From time to time the Governor and Council appointed special justices of this Court, in causes in which one or more of the standing justices were interested. A list of these appointments is here given.]

DATE OF APPOINTMENT.		SPECIAL JUSTICES.
1712.	Oct. 24.	Penn Townsend, Nathaniel Norden and John Burrill, in a certain cause.
1715.	Sept. 16.	Addington Davenport and Thomas Hutchinson, in a certain cause.
1718–9.	Jan. 7.	John Clark and Thomas Fitch, in a certain cause.
1719.	June 27.	John Clark and Thomas Fitch, in place of Sewall and Lynde, in all causes where John Leverett or Stephen Sewall on the one side, and Edmund Goffe on the other, may be concerned.
1720.	Dec. 15.	Josiah Wolcott, in place of T. Fitch, in same causes.
1723.	Sept. 6.	John Cushing, John Clarke and Jonathan Remington, in all causes wherein the proprietors of the town of Dorchester are parties.
1725.	Dec. 10.	Thomas Fitch, "in a cause commenced by Samuel Sewall, Chief Justice of said Court, as he is a Judge of Probate of Wills for the county of Suffolk," against John Langdon of Boston.
1726.	Sept. 1.	Job Almy, in the place of Paul Dudley, in causes against Nathaniel Halloway and Capt. Josiah Winslow of Freetown.
1726–7.	Feb. 23.	Elisha Cooke and Jonathan Remington, in a cause named.
1727.	June 19.	Isaac Winslow and John Cushing, in a cause named.
	June 27.	Nathaniel Byfield, Thomas Fitch and Jonathan Remington, in a cause named.
1728.	Dec. 12.	Nathaniel Byfield and Thomas Fitch, in place of Lynde and Quincy, in the cause of John Guild and Nathaniel Brewer.

Special Justices of the Superior Court—Continued.

DATE OF APPOINTMENT.		SPECIAL JUSTICES.
1728.	Dec. 12.	Thomas Fitch, Theophilus Burrill and Jonathan Remington, in place of Lynde, Davenport and Quincy, in certain causes.
	Dec. 19.	Nathaniel Byfield and Adam Winthrop, in a cause named.
1732–3.	Jan. 11.	Nathaniel Byfield, in the place of Lynde, in a cause named.
1733.	June 22.	Adam Winthrop and Thomas Cushing, in the place of Dudley and Remington, in two causes referring to the Great Bridge.
	June 22.	Adam Winthrop, Thomas Cushing and Ezekiel Lewis, in the place of Lynde, Dudley and Remington, in a cause mentioned.
1735.	Apr. 19.	Theophilus Burrill and Joseph Wilder, for the county of York.
	June 27.	Samuel Thaxter and Thomas Berry, in the place of Davenport and Dudley, in all causes in which the inhabitants of Boston are concerned.
	June 27.	Benjamin Prescott, in the county of Worcester, in the place of Dudley.
1736–7.	Feb. 10.	Thomas Greaves, in the place of Dudley, in the causes of Samuel Shute and John Yeamans, of London, against Benjamin Pemberton; and between Benjamin Bronsden, William Bant and Mercy Frizzell, executors of John Frizzell.
1737.	Oct. 25.	Job Almy, in place of Dudley, in a cause.
	Nov. 10.	Thomas Greaves, in place of Dudley, in a cause.
		Benjamin Prescott, in place of Dudley, in a cause.
1738.	Aug. 12.	Seth Williams and Benjamin Marston, in certain causes.
	Aug. 19.	William Ward, in the place of Greaves, in a cause.
1738–9.	Mar. 2.	Seth Williams and William Ward, in certain causes.
1739.	May 2.	Edward Hutchinson, Joseph Wilder and Stephen Sewall, in certain causes.
	June 15.	Ebenezer Burrill, in certain causes.
1739–40.	Jan. 24.	Thomas Berry and Benjamin Marston, in a cause.
1743.	Apr. 18.	Edward Hutchinson and Nathaniel Hubbard, in a cause.
	Nov. 3.	Edward Hutchinson and Nathaniel Hubbard, in a certain cause.
1744.	Oct. 23.	John Cushing and Sylvanus Bourne, in a cause.

Special Justices of the Superior Court—Continued.

DATE OF APPOINTMENT.		SPECIAL JUSTICES.
1747.	Aug. 19.	John Cushing, Sylvanus Bourne and Joseph Pynchon, in the place of Saltonstall, Hubbard and Lynde, in all causes relating to the Silver Bank, they being partners.
1748.	Apr. 6.	John Greenleaf, special, in all causes relating to land titles in York.
1748–9.	Jan. 11.	Ezekiel Cheever and Chambers Russell, in place of Saltonstall and Sewall, in a cause named.
	Mar. 2.	John Jeffries, William Brattle and Thomas Hubbard, in place of Saltonstall, Sewall and Lynde, in the cause of the Silver Bank.
1749.	June 19.	Joseph Sawyer and Nathaniel Sparhawk, at York, in causes where a quorum of the standing justices is not present.
	Aug. 12.	Ezekiel Cheever and Joseph Richards, in causes in which the town of Boston is concerned.
1749–50.	Feb. 23.	Chambers Russell and Simon Frost, in a special Court of Assize at York, in place of Lynde and Cushing.
1753.	Aug. 24.	Samuel Danforth and Ezekiel Cheever, in causes relative to the town of Boston.
1754.	Sept. 20.	Thomas Hutchinson, in place of John Cushing, in the cause of William Vassal of Boston.
1755.	Feb. 21.	Thomas Hutchinson, in the place of Cushing, in a certain cause.
	June 26.	William Brattle, in a cause named.
1756.	Feb. 13.	Andrew Oliver and William Brattle, in William Vassal's cause.
	Feb. 20.	John Chandler and Andrew Oliver, in certain causes.
1758.	Aug. 1.	Benjamin Lincoln and Samuel White, in place of Cushing and Russell, in any cause relating to the validity of the will of Gov. Bellingham.
1762.	Feb. 23.	Timothy Ruggles, in the place of Russell, in a cause named.
	Aug. 19.	Samuel Danforth, in place of Russell, in a cause named.
1768.	Apr. 11.	Foster Hutchinson, in a cause named.
	Sept. 7.	Nathaniel Ropes, in a cause named.
1770.	Aug. 30.	Nathaniel Ropes and Joseph Lee, in a certain cause.

Special Justices of the Superior Court—Concluded.

DATE OF APPOINTMENT.		SPECIAL JUSTICES.
1770.	Sept. 17.	Jedidiah Foster, special, in a certain cause.
1771.	Feb. 14.	Timothy Pain, special, in a certain cause.
1773.	Feb. 17.	Joseph Lee and William Browne, in certain causes.
	Mar. 4.	Joseph Lee and William Browne, in certain causes.

COMMISSIONERS OF OYER AND TERMINER.*

DATE OF APPOINTMENT.		COMMISSIONERS.
1692.	June 13.	William Stoughton, John Richards, Nathaniel Saltonstall, Wait Winthrop, Bartholomew Gedney, Samuel Sewall, John Hathorne, Jonathan Corwin and Peter Sergeant, or any five of them, to enquire of, hear and determine all manner of crimes and offences perpetrated within the counties of Suffolk, Essex and Middlesex, or of either of them.
	July 26.	Anthony Checkley was appointed to officiate as Attorney for and in behalf of their Majesties in the special Court of Oyer and Terminer, and Thomas Newton also as their Majesties Attorney. Capt. Stephen Sewall was made Clerk of this Court. This was the Court which tried the Salem witchcraft causes.
	Oct. 22.	Francis Hooke, Charles Frost, Samuel Wheelwright and Thomas Newton, justices to enquire of, hear and determine all murders, &c., perpetrated within the County of York.
1698.	Dec. 22.	Thomas Danforth, Wait Winthrop, Elisha Cooke and Samuel Sewall, for the trial of Jacob Smith.
1703.	Nov. 23.	John Hathorne, William Browne, Jonathan Corwin, Benjamin Browne and John Higginson, for the trial of an Indian at Salem.
1704.	June 15.	John Gardner, James Cotlin, Thomas Mayhew, Benjamin Skiffe and William Gayer, for the trial of an Indian at Nantucket.
1707.	Nov. 8.	Joseph Hammond, Ichabod Plaisted, John Plaisted, William Pepperrell, John Wheelwright, Capt. John Hill and Capt. Lewis Bane, or any four of them, for the trial of Joseph Gunnison for killing Grace Wentworth.
1711.	Mar. 7.	Wait Winthrop, Samuel Sewall, John Hathorne, Jonathan Corwin and Elisha Hutchinson, (Winthrop or Sewall to be one.)

* Appointed by the Governor and Council.

Commissioners of Oyer and Terminer—Concluded.

DATE OF APPOINTMENT.	COMMISSIONERS.
1713. June 5.	Nathaniel Thomas, John Otis, James Warren and John Gorham, or any three of them, (Thomas being one,) to try two Indians in Barnstable, for capital offences.
1718. Dec. 3.	Samuel Partridge, John Pynchon, Joseph Parsons and John Stoddard, for the trial at Northampton of Ovid Ruchbrock, for counterfeiting the public bills of credit of this Province and the Colony of Connecticut.
1743. June 23.	John Cushing, Sylvanus Bourne, Zaccheus Mayhew, Enoch Coffin and John Otis, for the trial of an Indian at Nantucket.
1746. Aug. 9.	John Cushing, Sylvanus Bourne, Zaccheus Mayhew, Enoch Coffin and John Otis, at a Court at Nantucket.

SUFFOLK COUNTY.

INFERIOR COURT OF COMMON PLEAS.

DATE OF APPOINTMENT.		NAMES.
1692.	Dec. 7.	Elisha Hutchinson, Peter Sergeant, John Foster, and Isaac Addington appointed.
		Hutchinson, Sergeant, Foster, Addington.
1696.	Oct. 16.	The same re-appointed.
1699.	July 17.	The same re-appointed.
1702.	June 29.	Elisha Hutchinson and John Foster appointed.[1]
	July 2.	Jeremiah Dummer appointed.[2]
	Aug. 14.	Penn Townsend appointed.[2]
		Hutchinson, Foster, Dummer, Townsend.
1711.	June 11.	Thomas Palmer, appointed.[3]
		Hutchinson, Dummer, Townsend, Palmer.
1715.	Dec. 9.	Elisha Hutchinson, Thomas Palmer, Edward Lyde and Adam Winthrop appointed.[4]
		Hutchinson, Palmer, Lyde, Winthrop.
1718.	Apr. 16.	Penn Townsend appointed.[5]
		Townsend, Palmer, Lyde, Winthrop.
1722–3.	Mch. 20.	Edward Hutchinson appointed.[6]
		Townsend, Palmer, Winthrop, Hutchinson.
1727.	Dec. 26.	William Dudley appointed.[7]
		Palmer, Winthrop, Hutchinson, Dudley.
1728.	Dec. 19.	Same confirmed.

[1] June 29, 1702. Thomas Brattle and Samuel Legg were nominated also, but rejected. Addington had been promoted to the Superior Court, and Sergeant was dropped.

[2] Nathaniel Oliver was also nominated, July 2, 1702, but was rejected. July 8th. Thomas Brattle was again nominated and rejected.

[3] John Foster having died Feb. 9, 1710–11, the Governor nominated, March 23, 1710–11, Thomas Brattle, who was rejected. He then, April 2, 1711, nominated Samuel Lynde, who was rejected: and the Council added, " It is their unanimous opinion That the three surviving Justices, being a Quorum according to the Law, are legally qualified to hold the said Court, and ought to hold the same accordingly, that the service of the Queen nor subjects be prejudiced for failure thereof." Palmer was finally appointed.

[4] Dummer and Townsend were omitted, the former probably on account of his age, 70 years.

[5] Elisha Hutchinson had died, Dec. 10, 1717, and Townsend was recalled to the bench to take his place as Chief Justice.

[6] Edward Hutchinson was appointed " in the place of Edward Lyde."

[7] Penn Townsend died Aug. 21, 1727, making this vacancy.

Inferior Court of Common Pleas—Continued.

DATE OF APPOINTMENT.	NAMES.
1731. Dec. 29.	Nathaniel Byfield, Elisha Cooke, Thomas Palmer and Adam Winthrop appointed.[8]
	Byfield, Cooke, Palmer, Winthrop.
1733. June 21.	Thomas Palmer, Adam Winthrop, William Dudley and Anthony Stoddard appointed.[9]
	Palmer, Winthrop, Dudley, Stoddard.
1740. Oct. 27.	Edward Hutchinson appointed.[10]
	Winthrop, Dudley, Stoddard, Hutchinson.
1741. Dec. 31.	Eliakim Hutchinson appointed.[11]
	Dudley, Stoddard, Hutchinson, Hutchinson.
1743. Oct. 20.	Edward Winslow appointed.[12]
	Ed. Hutchinson, Stoddard, Elm. Hutchinson, Winslow.
1748. Apr. 6.	Samuel Watts appointed.[13]
	Ed. Hutchinson, El. Hutchinson, Winslow, Watts.
1752. Apr. 3.	Thomas Hutchinson appointed.[14]
	Elm. Hutchinson, Winslow, Watts, T. Hutchinson.
1755. Jan. 8.	Samuel Welles appointed.[15]
	Elm. Hutchinson, Watts, T. Hutchinson, Welles.
1758. Apr. 1.	Foster Hutchinson appointed.[16]
	Elm. Hutchinson, Watts, Welles, F. Hutchinson.
1761. Nov. 5.	The same confirmed.
1770. May 9.	William Reed appointed.[17]
	Elm. Hutchinson, Welles, F. Hutchinson, Reed.
1771. Jan. 10.	Nathaniel Hatch appointed.[18]
	Elm. Hutchinson, F. Hutchinson, Reed, Hatch.

[8] Hutchinson and Dudley were both displaced at this appointment, though both afterwards were returned.

[9] Thomas Palmer was promoted to the place of Nathaniel Byfield, who died 6 June, 1733; Winthrop to Cooke's place; Dudley returned to the bench, and Stoddard was a new appointment.

[10] Edward Hutchinson filled the vacancy caused by the death of Thomas Palmer, Oct. 8th, 1740.

[11] Eliakim Hutchinson was in the place of Adam Winthrop, resigned.

[12] Edward Winslow was appointed to fill the vacancy caused by the death of William Dudley, Aug. 10th, 1743.

[13] Samuel Watts was in the place of Stoddard, who died March 11, 1748.

[14] Thomas Hutchinson succeeded his uncle Edward H., who died March 16, 1742.

[15] Welles succeeded Winslow, who died Dec., 1753, aged 85.

[16] Thomas Hutchinson having resigned "on account of his several employments," his brother succeeded him.

[17] William Reed took the place of Watts, who died March 12, 1770.

[18] Hatch succeeded Welles, who died May 20, 1770.

Inferior Court of Common Pleas—Concluded.

DATE OF APPOINTMENT.		NAMES.
1772.	July 3.	Eliakim Hutchinson, "*First Justice*," William Reed, Nathaniel Hatch and Joseph Green appointed.[19]
		Elia. Hutchinson, Reed, Hatch, Green.
1772.	Dec. 31.	Thomas Hutchinson, Jr., appointed.[20]
		Elia. Hutchinson, Reed, Hatch, T. Hutchinson, Jr.

SPECIAL JUSTICES COURT OF COMMON PLEAS.[21]

1725.	Dec. 18.	Samuel Checkley and Anthony Stoddard.
1731–2.	Feb. 3.	Anthony Stoddard, Francis Fulham, Thomas Greaves and Hugh Hall.
1734.	Dec. 31.	Josiah Quincy.
1734–5.	Feb. 21.	Samuel Danforth, Francis Foxcroft and Francis Fulham.
1748.	April 6.	John Quincy and James Minot.
1770.	Jan. 24.	Benjamin Lincoln and Joseph Williams.

SHERIFFS.

1692.	May 27.	Samuel Gookin.
1700–1.	Mch. 6.	Duncan Campbell named and rejected.
1702.	Oct. 23.	Giles Dye.
1713.	Aug. 27.	Lt. Col. William Dudley, "in room of Dyer, deceased."
1714–15.	Feb. 19.	William Payne, acting sheriff.
	Mch. 21.	William Dudley restored.
1715.	Dec. 9.	William Payne.
1728.	Dec. 12.	Edward Winslow.
1732.	Dec. 15.	Edward Winslow.
1743.	Oct. 20.	Benjamin Pollard.
1757.	Jan. 3.	Stephen Greenleaf.
1761.	Nov. 5.	Stephen Greenleaf.

[19] Green here first appears; yet Foster Hutchinson had been promoted to the Superior Court, March 21, 1771. Possibly there was a vacancy for some fifteen months.

[20] Thomas Hutchinson, Jr., took the place of Green.

[21] Appointed to act in cases in which any of the standing justices were interested.

JUDGES OF PROBATE.

DATE OF APPOINTMENT.	NAMES.
1692. June 18.	William Stoughton.
1701. Aug. 8.	Elisha Cooke.
1702. Nov. 19.	Isaac Addington.
1715. Dec. 9.	Samuel Sewall.
1728. Dec. 19.	Josiah Willard.
1741. Nov. 5.	Josiah Willard.
1745–6. Feb. 12.	Edward Hutchinson, in the place of Willard, resigned.
1752. April 3.	Thomas Hutchinson.
1761. Nov. 5.	Thomas Hutchinson.
1769. Aug. 3.	Foster Hutchinson, to the Revolution.

REGISTERS OF PROBATE.

1692. June 18.	Isaac Addington.
1702. Nov. 19.	Paul Dudley.
1715. Dec. 19.	Joseph Marion. John Boydell.
1722. Oct. 19.	Benj. Rolfe, "in the room of John Boydell, and during his absence."[1]
1728. Dec. 19.	John Boydell.
1732. Dec. 15.	John Boydell.
1739. Dec. 21.	Andrew Belcher, "in place of J. Boydell, deceased."
1741. Nov. 5.	Andrew Belcher.
1749. July 14.	John Payne, in the absence of Belcher from the Province.
1754. Jan. 25.	John Shirley, "in place of Andrew Belcher."
Sept. 20.	John Payne "for the space of three months from this Time, or until the return of John Shirley, if it be before three months be expired."

[1] 1725. Feb. 23. Rolfe was to act in Boydell's place in the case of the estate of Thomas Lewis, to whom Boydell was related.

Registers of Probate—Concluded.

DATE OF APPOINTMENT.	NAMES.
1755. Jan. 11.	John Payne continued for two months if Shirley remain absent.
Mch. 28.	John Payne, ⎫ Joint Registers, in the place of John Shirley, John Cotton, ⎭ who had resigned.
1759. Dec. 19.	William Cooper, ⎫ Joint Registers. John Cotton, ⎭
1761. Nov. 5.	William Cooper, ⎫ Joint Registers. John Cotton, ⎭

ESSEX COUNTY.

INFERIOR COURT OF COMMON PLEAS.

DATE OF APPOINTMENT.	NAMES.
1692. Dec. 7.	Bartholomew Gedney, Samuel Appleton, John Hathorne and Jonathan Corwin appointed.
	Gedney, Appleton, Hathorne, Corwin.
1696. June 4.	Bartholomew Gedney, John Hathorne, William Browne and Jonathan Corwin appointed.[1]
	Gedney, Hathorne, Browne, Corwin.
1698. June 3.	Daniel Peirce appointed.[2]
	Hathorne, Browne, Corwin, Peirce.
1699. July 17.	The same confirmed.
1702. June 30.	Nathaniel Saltonstall, William Browne, John Hathorne and Daniel Peirce appointed.
	Saltonstall, Browne, Hathorne, Peirce.
Oct. 23.	Jonathan Corwin appointed.[3]
	Saltonstall, Browne, Peirce, Corwin.
1704. June 14.	John Appleton appointed.[4]
	Saltonstall, Browne, Corwin, Appleton.
1707. June 10.	Thomas Noyes appointed.[5]
	Appleton, Browne, Corwin, Noyes.
1708. June 15.	John Higginson appointed.[6]
	Appleton, Browne, Noyes, Higginson.
1715. Dec. 9.	John Appleton, John Higginson, Thomas Noyes and Samuel Browne appointed.[7]
	Appleton, Higginson, Noyes, Browne.

[1] William Browne in place of Samuel Appleton, who died May 15, 1696. Oct. 16, same continued.

[2] Daniel Peirce appointed "in the place of Bartholomew Gedney, deceased," who died Feb. 28, 1697-8.

[3] It seems that Corwin had been superseded by Saltonstall at the time of appointments in June: but as Hathorne was appointed to the Superior Court Aug. 14th, Corwin was re-instated very soon.

[4] John Appleton was in place of Daniel Peirce, who died Jan. 22, 1703-4.

[5] Thomas Noyes was in place of Nathaniel Saltonstall, who died May 21, 1707.

[6] Higginson filled the vacancy caused by Corwin's appointment to the Superior Court.

[7] William Browne, being old, (he died Feb. 14, 1715-16, aged 78,) was replaced at this time by his son, Samuel.

Inferior Court of Common Pleas—Continued.

DATE OF APPOINTMENT.	NAMES.
1720. July 15.	John Burrill appointed.[8]
	Appleton, Noyes, Browne, Burrill.
1721-2. Mch. 9.	Josiah Wolcott appointed.[9]
	Appleton, Noyes, Browne, Wolcott.
1729. April 10.	John Appleton, Samuel Browne, Timothy Lindall and John Wainwright appointed.[10]
	Appleton, Browne, Lindall, Wainwright.
1733. June 21.	Timothy Lindall, Theophilus Burrill, John Wainwright and Thomas Berry appointed.[11]
	Lindall, Burrill, Wainwright, Berry.
1737. Nov. 10.	Benjamin Marston appointed.[12]
	Lindall, Wainwright, Berry, Marston.
1739. Oct. 5.	Benjamin Lynde, Jr., appointed.[13]
	Lindall, Berry, Marston, Lynde.
1745-6. Feb. 8.	John Choat appointed.[14]
	Lindall, Berry, Marston, Choat.
1754. Jan. 25.	Henry Gibbs appointed.[15]
	Berry, Marston, Choat, Gibbs.
Apr. 20.	John Tasker appointed.[16]
	Berry, Choat, Gibbs, Tasker.
1756. Sept. 14.	Benjamin Pickman appointed.[17]
	Choat, Gibbs, Tasker, Pickman.
1759. Mch. 8.	Caleb Cushing appointed.[18]
	Choat, Tasker, Pickman, Cushing.

[8] John Burrill was in place of John Higginson, who died 23d Mch. 1719-20.

[9] Wolcott was in place of John Burrill, who died Dec. 10th, 1721.

[10] Thomas Noyes (who died April 12, 1730,) was very old, and hence probably omitted. Josiah Wolcott had died Feb. 2, 1728-9. There were, therefore, two new appointments at this time.

[11] Samuel Browne had died June 16, 1731. John Appleton was probably omitted on the score of his age, 80 years, though he was continued in the Probate Court.

[12] Marston was in the place of Theophilus Burrill, who died 4th July, 1747.

[13] Lynde succeeded John Wainwright, who died Sept. 1, 1739.

[14] Choat was appointed when Benjamin Lynde was transferred to the Superior Court.

[15] Gibbs was in the place of " Timothy Lindall, who had resigned."

[16] Tasker succeeded Marston, who died 22d May, 1754, aged 57.

[17] Pickman succeeded Berry, who died 10th August, 1756.

[18] Cushing took the place of Gibbs, who died Feb., 1759.

Inferior Court of Common Pleas—Concluded.

DATE OF APPOINTMENT.		NAMES.
1761.	June 24.	Stephen Higginson appointed.[19]
		Choat, Tasker, Cushing, Higginson.
	Nov. 19.	Nathaniel Ropes and Andrew Oliver appointed.[20]
		Choat, Cushing, Ropes, Oliver.
1766.	Feb. 5.	William Bourn appointed.[21]
		Ropes, Cushing, Oliver, Bourn.
1770.	Sept. 17.	William Browne appointed.[22]
		Ropes, Cushing, Oliver, Browne.
1772.	Jan. 15.	Peter Frye appointed.[23]
		Cushing, Oliver, Browne, Frye.

SPECIAL JUSTICES COURT OF COMMON PLEAS.

1711.	Oct. 26.	Samuel Appleton and John Burrill.
1715.	Sept. 16.	Samuel Appleton and John Burrill.
1725.	Sept. 30.	John Wainwright and Theophilus Burrill.
1729.	April 11.	Theophilus Burrill and William Gedney.
	July 3.	Theophilus Burrill and William Gedney.
1731.	Aug. 25.	Theophilus Burrill and Richard Kent.
1734.	June 28.	Nathaniel Coffin and Benjamin Lynde, Jr.
1740.	July 5.	Epes Sergeant and Daniel Appleton.
1744.	Aug. 18.	Epes Sergeant and Daniel Appleton.
1744–5.	Jan. 19.	John Choat.
1755.	Mch. 28.	John Greenleaf.
1762.	Mch. 11.	Epes Sergeant and Daniel Appleton.
1763.	Feb. 17.	Jacob Fowle and Samuel Rogers.
1766.	Feb. 5.	William Brown.

[19] Higginson is named in the place of Pickman, in a new commission of this date. He died, however, Oct. 12, 1761, aged 45.

[20] Ropes and Oliver are named in the new commission of this date, in the place of Higginson, deceased Oct. 12, 1761, and Tasker, who died Nov. 9, 1761.

[21] Bourn was to fill the vacancy caused by the death of Choat, and Ropes was at the same date made Chief Justice.

[22] Browne succeeded Bourn, who died Aug. 12, 1770, aged 47.

[23] Frye succeeded Ropes, transferred to the Superior Court.

SHERIFFS.

DATE OF APPOINTMENT.	NAMES.
1692. May 27.	Capt. George Corwin.
1696. Apr. 23.	William Gedney.
1702. July 2.	Major Francis Wainwright.
Oct. 23.	William Gedney.[1] / Major Daniel Denison.
1708–9. Feb. 25.	Major Daniel Denison.
1710. June 30.	William Gedney.
1715. Sept. 16.	John Denison.
Dec. 9.	William Gedney, / John Denison, } Joint Sheriffs.
1722. July 3.	Benjamin Marston, / John Denison, } Joint Sheriffs.
1728. Dec. 12.	Benjamin Marston.
1733. June 22.	Benjamin Marston.
1745–6. Jan. 24.	Robert Hale.
1761. June 24.	Robert Hale.
Nov. 19.	Robert Hale.
1766. Aug. 6.	Richard Saltonstall.

[1] 1708, June 16. Denison was suspended, and "the county continued at present in the keeping of Mr. William Gedney, the other sheriff, he to make a deputy at Ipswich and another at Newbury."

JUDGES AND REGISTERS OF PROBATE.

DATE OF APPOINTMENT.	JUDGES.	DATE OF APPOINTMENT.	REGISTERS.
1692. June 18.	Bartholomew Gedney.	1692. June 18.	Stephen Sewell.
1698. June 3.	Jonathan Corwin.	1695. Nov. 29.	John Croade.
1702. Oct. 23.	John Appleton.	1698. June 3.	John Higginson.
1715. Dec. 9.	John Appleton.	1702. Oct. 23.	Daniel Rogers.
1729. Apr. 11.	John Appleton.	1715. Dec. 29.	Daniel Rogers.
1733. June 22.	John Appleton.	1722–3. Jan. 9.	Daniel Appleton.
1739. Oct. 5.	Thomas Berry.	1729. Apr. 11.	Daniel Appleton.
1746. Aug. 5.	Thomas Berry.	1733. June 22.	Daniel Appleton.
1756. Sept. 14.	John Choate.	1761. June 24.	Daniel Appleton.
1761. June 24.	John Choate.	Nov. 19.	Daniel Appleton.
Nov. 19.	John Choate.	1762. Aug. 26.	Samuel Rogers.
1766. Feb. 5.	Nathaniel Ropes.	1773. Sept. 29.	Peter Frye.
1772. Jan. 15.	Benjamin Lynde.		

MIDDLESEX COUNTY.

INFERIOR COURT OF COMMON PLEAS.

DATE OF APPOINTMENT.		NAMES.
1692.	Dec. 7.	John Phillips, James Russell, Joseph Lynde and Samuel Hayman appointed.
		Phillips, Russell, Lynde, Hayman.
1696.	Oct. 16.	The same confirmed.
1699.	July 17.	The same confirmed.
1702.	June 29.	James Russell, John Phillips and Jonathan Tyng appointed.[1]
	July 8.	Joseph Lynde appointed.
		Russell, Phillips, Tyng, Lynde.
1709.	June 23.	Francis Foxcroft appointed.[2]
		Phillips, Tyng, Lynde, Foxcroft.
1715.	Dec. 9.	Joseph Lynde, Francis Foxcroft, Jonathan Tyng and Jonathan Remington appointed.[3]
		Lynde, Foxcroft, Tyng, Remington.
1719.	June 27.	Jonathan Dowse, Charles Chambers and Francis Fulham appointed.[4]
		Remington, Dowse, Chambers, Fulham.
1729.	Aug. 22.	The same confirmed.
1731.	July 9.	The same confirmed.
1733.	June 22.	Thomas Greaves appointed.[5]
		Dowse, Chambers, Fulham, Greaves.
1737-8.	Mch. 9.	Francis Foxcroft appointed.[6]
		Dowse, Chambers, Fulham, Foxcroft.

---

[1] Samuel Hayman, thus superseded, died Dec., 1712, aged 73.

[2] Foxcroft was appointed, owing to the death of James Russell, April 28, 1709.

[3] Remington was a new appointment. Phillips, probably, was omitted on account of his age, 83 years, though he lived until Mch. 29, 1724-5.

[4] Dowse, Chambers and Fulham were appointed in the room of Lynde, Tyng and Foxcroft. Very probably these three were dropped on account of their age, Lynde (who died Jany. 29, 1727) being then 82, Tyng, 77 (he died Jany. 19, 1724), and Foxcroft (who died Jany. 1728), 62 years.

[5] Greaves succeeded Jonathan Remington, who was transferred to the Supreme Court.

[6] Foxcroft was appointed Mch. 9 " in the room of Thomas Greaves, Esq., while he remains one of the Justices of the Superior Court," and Aug. 19 he was regularly appointed.

Inferior Court of Common Pleas—Concluded.

DATE OF APPOINTMENT.		NAMES.
1739.	Dec. 21.	Thomas Greaves re-appointed.[7]
		Dowse, Fulham, Greaves, Foxcroft.
1741.	July 21.	Samuel Danforth appointed.[8]
		Fulham, Greaves, Foxcroft, Danforth.
1747.	Aug. 19.	Chambers Russell appointed.[9]
		Fulham, Foxcroft, Danforth, Russell.
1752.	April 7.	Andrew Boardman appointed.[10]
		Fulham, Foxcroft, Danforth, Boardman.
1753.	Aug. 24.	Same four confirmed.
1755.	June 26.	William Lawrence appointed.[11]
		Foxcroft, Danforth, Boardman, Lawrence.
1761.	Nov. 20.	Same confirmed.
1763.	Sept. 7.	John Tyng appointed.[12]
		Danforth, Foxcroft, Boardman, Tyng.
1764.	Mch. 7.	Richard Foster appointed.[13]
		Danforth, Boardman, Tyng, Foster.
1769.	May 24.	Joseph Lee appointed.[14]
		Danforth, Tyng, Foster, Lee.
1771.	May 16.	James Russell appointed.[15]
		Danforth, Tyng, Lee, Russell.
		Last term of the Court was held May 21, 1774.

[7] Greaves was superseded on the bench of the Superior Court by Stephen Sewall, May 16, 1739. He was reappointed here "in the room of Charles Chambers, Esq., who had resigned," and Foxcroft's appointment remained undisturbed. Chambers was old, being 82 at his death, 27 Apr., 1743.

[8] Danforth was "in the room of Jonathan Dowse, Esq.," who was then probably too old to serve longer, being 82 at his death, 28 Jany., 1744–5.

[9] Russell succeeded Greaves, who died 19 June, 1747.

[10] Boardman took the place of Russell, promoted to Superior Court.

[11] Lawrence succeeded Francis Fulham, who resigned, and died 18 Jany., 1758, aged 87.

[12] Tyng, no doubt, succeeded Lawrence, who probably resigned before his death, May 19, 1764, aged 67.

[13] Foster succeeded Foxcroft, who probably resigned this year, and died Mch. 28, 1768, aged 75.

[14] Lee was to fill the vacancy caused by the death of Boardman, May 20, 1769.

[15] Russell succeeded Foster, who resigned, and died Aug. 1774, aged 82.

SPECIAL JUSTICES COURT OF COMMON PLEAS.

DATE OF APPOINTMENT.		NAMES.
1705.	June 8.	Elisha Hutchinson, John Foster and John Higginson.
1708.	Feb. 25.	Elisha Hutchinson, John Foster, Penn Townsend and Jonathan Tyng.
1718.	Dec. 3.	Jonathan Dowse and Jonas Bond.
1719.	Nov. 25.	Nathaniel Carey, Spencer Phips and Thomas Greaves.
1723.	Sept. 6.	Spencer Phips and Jonas Bond.
1726.	June 18.	Spencer Phips, Henry Phillips and Francis Foxcroft, Jr.
1729.	Aug. 3.	Henry Phillips.
1729–30.	Mch. 19.	Francis Foxcroft.
1731.	July 9.	Spencer Phips, Thomas Greaves and Francis Foxcroft.
1732.	Dec. 15.	Habijah Savage, Samuel Wells and Samuel Danforth.
1736.	Dec. 29.	Jacob Wendell and Benjamin Prescott.
1741.	July 25.	Simon Tufts and Ephraim Curtis.
1749.	Aug. 12.	William Lawrence.
1751.	June 21.	William Lawrence.
1762.	July 29.	John Tyng and Oliver Fletcher.
1764.	Mch. 7.	Joseph Lee.
1768.	Sept. 7.	Samuel Livermore and Charles Prescott.

SHERIFFS.

1692.	May 27.	Timothy Phillips.	1729.	Sept. 27.	Samuel Dummer.
1702.	Oct. 23.	Samuel Gookin.	1731.	July 9.	Richard Foster, Jr.
1715.	Dec. 9.	Edmund Goffe.	1761.	Nov. 20.	Richard Foster.
1728.	Dec. 12.	Samuel Gookin.	1764.	Mch. 7.	David Phips.

JUDGES AND REGISTERS OF PROBATE.

DATE OF APPOINTMENT.	JUDGES.	DATE OF APPOINTMENT.	REGISTERS.
1692. June 18.	James Russell.	1692. June 18.	Samuel Phipps.
1702. Oct. 23.	John Leverett.	1702. Oct. 23.	Thomas Swan.
1708. July 8.	Francis Foxcroft.	1705. Sept. 15.	Nicholas Fessenden.
1715. Dec. 9.	Francis Foxcroft.	1709. Dec. 28.	Daniel Foxcroft.
1725. Sept. 30.	Jonathan Remington.	1715. Dec. 9.	Thomas Foxcroft.
1729. July 3.	Jonathan Remington.	1729. July 3.	Francis Foxcroft.
1731. July 9.	Jonathan Remington.	1731. July 9.	Samuel Danforth.
1745. Dec. 20.	Samuel Danforth.	1745. Dec. 20.	Andrew Boardman, Jr.
1761. Nov. 20.	Samuel Danforth.	1753. Aug. 10.	Andrew Boardman.
		1769. May 29.	William Kneeland.

[NOTE.—Jan. 1 and Aug. 12, 1772, Andrew Boardman was made special register, to complete his father's record.]

HAMPSHIRE COUNTY.

COURT OF COMMON PLEAS.

DATE OF APPOINTMENT.		NAMES.
1692.	Dec. 7.	John Pynchon, Peter Tilton, Samuel Partridge, Joseph Hawley appointed.
		Pynchon, Tilton, Partridge, Hawley.
1696.	Oct. 16.	John Pynchon, Samuel Partridge, Joseph Hawley, Joseph Parsons appointed.[1]
		J. Pynchon, (1st,) Partridge, Hawley, Parsons.
1699.	July 17.	Same four confirmed.
1702.	June 29.	Same four confirmed.
1710.	June 8.	John Pynchon appointed.[2]
		Partridge, Hawley, Parsons, J. Pynchon, (2d.)
1711.	June 8.	Samuel Porter appointed.[3]
		Partridge, Parsons, J. Pynchon, (2d.)
1715.	Dec. 10.	Same four confirmed.
1719.	June 27.	John Stoddard appointed.[4]
		Partridge, J. Pynchon, (2d.) Porter, Stoddard.
1722.	June 29.	John Pynchon appointed.[5]
		Partridge, Porter, Stoddard, J. Pynchon, (3d.)
1722-3.	Jan. 9.	Henry Dwight, John Ashley appointed.[6]
		Partridge, Stoddard, Dwight, Ashley.
1729.	Oct. 10.	Same four confirmed.
1732.	Dec. 28.	Samuel Partridge, John Stoddard, John Pynchon, (3d.) John Ashley appointed.[7]
		Partridge, Stoddard, J. Pynchon, (3d.) Ashley.

[1] Parsons succeeded Tilton, who died 11 July, 1696.

[2] J. Pynchon, (2d,) was appointed, "there being at present but three in that commission;" his father, John P., had died Jany. 17, 1702-3.

[3] Porter was appointed "to fill a vacancy;" Hawley having died   1711.

[4] Stoddard was "in room of Joseph Parsons," who lived till   Nov., 1729.

[5] John Pynchon, (3d,) was "in room of his father, deceased," who died 25 Apr., 1721.

[6] Dwight and Ashley were "in the room of Samuel Porter and John Pynchon;" of these Porter had died 29 July, 1722, but Pynchon was superseded.

[7] John Pynchon, (3d,) was restored in place of Dwight, who died 20 Mch., 1731-2.

Court of Common Pleas—Continued.

DATE OF APPOINTMENT.	NAMES.
1734-5. Feb. 21.	Ebenezer Pomroy.[8]
	Partridge, Stoddard, Ashley, Pomroy.
1737. July 2.	John Stoddard, Eleazer Porter, Timothy Dwight, William Pynchon, Jr., appointed.[9]
	Stoddard, Porter, T. Dwight, W. Pynchon, Jr.
1738. July 8.	William Pynchon, Sr., appointed.[10]
	Stoddard, Porter, Dwight, W. Pynchon, Sr.
1741. Apr. 2.	Joseph Pynchon appointed.[11]
	Stoddard, Porter, Dwight, J. Pynchon.
July 21.	Ephraim Williams appointed.[12]
	Stoddard, Porter, J. Pynchon, Williams.
1748. Nov. 8.	Timothy Dwight appointed.[13]
	Porter, J. Pynchon, Williams, T. Dwight.
1749-50. Jan. 18.	Josiah Dwight appointed.[14]
	Porter, J. Pynchon, T. Dwight, J. Dwight.
1753. Jan. 4.	Joseph Dwight appointed.[15]
	Porter, T. Dwight, Josiah Dwight, Jos. Dwight.
1758. Jan. 11.	Joseph Dwight, Israel Williams, Josiah Dwight and Timothy Dwight, Jr., appointed.[16]
	Jos. Dwight, I. Williams, Josi. Dwight, T. Dwight, Jr.
1761. June 24.	Elijah Williams appointed.[17]
	I. Williams, Josi. Dwight, T. Dwight, Jr., E. Williams.

[8] Pomroy was "in the room of John Pynchon," thus again superseded, but who lived until 12 July, 1742, when he died, aged 68.

[9] Three new judges appointed; of those retired Partridge died 25 July, 1740, aged 95; Ashley died 17 Apr., 1759, aged 89; and Pomroy died   1754.

[10] Wm. Pynchon was "in room of Wm. Pynchon, Jr., who has resigned;" in this case an uncle succeeded his nephew.

[11] Joseph Pynchons succeeded Wm. P., Sr., who died 1 Jany., 1740-41, aged 52.

[12] Ephraim Williams was "in the room of Timothy Dwight," who lived long after this, dying 30 Apr., 1771.

[13] Timothy Dwight was restored after the death of Stoddard, 19 June, 1748.

[14] Josiah Dwight was "in the room of Ephraim Williams, resigned;" this was probably Ephraim W., Sr., who died in 1754, aged 63. Dwight seems to have been again commissioned Aug. 24 of same year.

[15] Joseph Dwight succeeded Joseph Pynchon; yet 17 Aug., 1753, Joseph Pynchon was named in the commission, and 13 Sept., 1753, Dwight is named in the commission instead. I conclude that this shows a clerical error in retaining Pynchon's name, which was promptly remedied by the Council.

[16] Israel Williams and Timothy Dwight, Jr., were new appointments: Porter died   1757, and Timothy Dwight undoubtedly resigned, as he lived till 10 July, 1771.

[17] Elijah Williams succeeded Joseph Dwight, who was transferred to Berkshire.

Court of Common Pleas—Concluded.

DATE OF APPOINTMENT.		NAMES.
1764.	Feb. 1.	Thomas Williams appointed.[18]
		I. Williams, J. Dwight, T. Dwight, T. Williams.
1768.	Oct. 26.	Israel Williams, Oliver Partridge, Timothy Dwight, Jr., Thomas Williams appointed.[19]
		I. Williams, Partridge, T. Dwight, Jr., T. Williams.

SPECIAL JUSTICES COURT OF COMMON PLEAS.

1721.	July 14.	Luke Hitchcock.
1727.	Dec. 26.	Eleazer Porter and Dr. Thomas Hastings.
1732-3.	Jan. 11.	Eleazer Porter and William Pynchon.
1738.	Aug. 19.	William Pynchon, Jr., and Israel Williams.
1753.	Sept. 13.	Elijah Williams.
1762.	Feb. 4.	Samuel Mather and Thomas Williams.
1764.	June 8.	Eleazer Porter.

SHERIFFS.

1692.	May 27.	Samuel Porter.
1702.	June 30.	Samuel Porter.
1707.	Dec. 5.	Luke Hitchcock.
1715.	Dec. 10.	Luke Hitchcock.
1719.	June 27.	Ebenezer Pomroy.
1728.	Dec. 12.	Ebenezer Pomroy.
1732.	Dec. 28.	Ebenezer Pomroy, Samuel Marshfield, } Joint Sheriffs.
1734-5.	Feb. 21.	Samuel Marshfield alone, Pomroy having resigned.
1740.	July 12.	Oliver Partridge, (in place of Marshfield, resigned.)
1749.	June 29.	Oliver Partridge.
1761.	June 24.	Oliver Partridge.
1768.	Oct. 26.	Solomon Stoddard.

[18] Thomas Williams succeeded Elijah Williams, who lived till 10 July, 1771.
[19] Oliver Partridge succeeded Josiah Dwight, who died 28 Sept., 1768.

JUDGES AND REGISTERS OF PROBATE.

DATE OF APPOINTMENT.	JUDGES.	DATE OF APPOINTMENT.	REGISTERS.
1692. June 18.	John Pynchon.	1692. June 18.	Samuel Partridge.
1702. Aug. 13.	John Pynchon.	1702. Aug. 13.	Samuel Partridge.
1702–3. Mch. 18.	Samuel Partridge.	1702–3. Mch. 18.	John Pynchon, Jr.
1715. Dec. 10.	Samuel Partridge.	1715. Dec. 10.	John Pynchon, Jr.
1729. July 10.	John Stoddard.	1729. July 10.	Timothy Dwight.
1732. Dec. 28.	John Stoddard.	1732. Dec. 28.	Timothy Dwight.
1748. Sept. 27.	Timothy Dwight.	1748. Sept. 27.	Timothy Dwight, Jr.
1753. Sept. 6.	Timothy Dwight.	1753. Sept. 6.	Timothy Dwight, Jr.
1758. June 22.	Timothy Dwight.	1758. June 22.	Timothy Dwight, Jr.
1761. June 24.	Timothy Dwight.	1761. June 24.	Timothy Dwight, Jr.
1764. June 8.	Israel Williams.	1764. June 8.	Timothy Dwight, Jr.* Solomon Stoddard.*
		1768. Oct. 26.	Israel Williams, Jr.

* Jointly.

PLYMOUTH COUNTY.

INFERIOR COURT OF COMMON PLEAS.

DATE OF APPOINTMENT.		NAMES.
1692.	Dec. 7.	William Bradford, Nathaniel Thomas, John Cushing and Ephraim Morton appointed.
		Bradford, Thomas, Cushing, Morton.
1696.	Oct. 16.	William Bradford, Nathaniel Thomas, John Wadsworth and Isaac Little appointed.[1]
		Bradford, Thomas, Wadsworth, Little.
1699.	July 17.	The same four confirmed.
1700.	June 7.	John Cushing, Jr., and James Warren appointed.[2]
		Bradford, Thomas, Cushing, Warren.
1702.	June 29.	Nathaniel Thomas, Isaac Winslow, John Cushing and James Warren appointed.[3]
		Thomas, Winslow, Cushing, Warren.
1702-3.	Mch. 18.	Joseph Otis appointed.[4]
		Thomas, Otis, Cushing, Warren.
1712.	June 4.	Isaac Winslow appointed.[5]
		Cushing, Otis, Warren, Winslow.
1715.	Dec. 9.	John Cushing, Isaac Winslow, Seth Arnold and Nathaniel Thomas, Jr., appointed.[6]
		Cushing, Winslow, Arnold, Thomas.
1721.	Nov. 15.	Isaac Lothrop appointed.[7]
		Cushing, Winslow, Thomas, Lothrop.

[1] Morton died 7 Sept., 1693; Cushing probably resigned, as he was then about 70 years old. He died 31 Mch., 1708.

[2] Little probably died 29 Dec., 1699, and Wadsworth died 15 May, 1700. These two vacancies were filled by new men.

[3] Winslow doubtless took the place of Bradford, who resigned, as he died 20 Feb., 1703-4, aged about 80 years.

[4] Otis seems to have taken the place of Winslow, since the latter was again appointed in 1712.

[5] Winslow took the place of Thomas, "transferred to the Superior Court."

[6] Arnold and Thomas succeeded Otis, who resigned, doubtless, as he lived till 1754, and Warren, who died May, 1715.

[7] Lothrop took the place of "Arnold, deceased."

Inferior Court of Common Pleas—Continued.

DATE OF APPOINTMENT.		NAMES.
1729.	April 10.	Isaac Winslow, Nathaniel Thomas, Isaac Lothrop and Josiah Cotton appointed.[8]
		Winslow, Thomas, Lothrop, Cotton.
1731.	Aug. 25.	Isaac Winslow, Nathaniel Thomas, Josiah Cotton and Nicholas Sever appointed.[9]
		Winslow, Thomas, Cotton, Sever.
1738.	July 8.	John Cushing appointed.[10]
		Thomas, Cotton, Sever, Cushing.
1738-9.	Mch. 1.	Isaac Lothrop appointed.[11]
		Lothrop, Cotton, Sever, Cushing.
1743.	Sept. 9.	Thomas Clapp appointed.[12]
		Sever, Cotton, Cushing, Clapp.
1747.	Dec. 12.	Peter Oliver appointed.[13]
		Sever, Cushing, Clapp, Oliver.
1747-8.	Mch. 1.	Isaac Lothrop appointed.[14]
		Sever, Clapp, Oliver, Lothrop, (2d.)
1751.	June 21.	Elijah Cushing appointed.[15]
		Sever, Clapp, Oliver, Cushing.
1756.	Sept. 14.	Thomas Foster appointed.[16]
		Sever, Clapp, Cushing, Foster.
1762.	Jan. 28.	John Winslow, Thomas Clapp, Elijah Cushing, Thomas Foster appointed.[17]
		Winslow, Clapp, Cushing, Foster.

[8] Cotton succeeded Cushing, who was "transferred to the Superior Court."
[9] Sever took the place of Lothrop, who was dropped for a few years, probably at his own request.
[10] John Cushing took the place of Isaac Winslow, who resigned.
[11] Lothrop was restored and made Chief Justice, in the room of N. Thomas, who died Feb., 1639, aged 75.
[12] Clapp was appointed after the death of Lothrop, 10 Sept., 1743, aged 70.
[13] Oliver was "in the room of Josiah Cotton, Esq., who had resigned."
[14] Isaac Lothrop, son of the former judge, took the place of Cushing, transferred to the Superior Court.
[15] Elijah Cushing was the successor of I. Lothrop, who died 26 Apr., 1750, aged 43.
[16] Foster was appointed as Oliver had been promoted to the Superior Court.
[17] Winslow was in the place of Sever, probably omitted on account of his age; he died Apr. 7, 1764, aged 81.

Inferior Court of Common Pleas—Concluded.

DATE OF APPOINTMENT.		NAMES.
1762.	Aug. 19.	Gamaliel Bradford appointed.[18]
		Winslow, Clapp, Foster, Bradford.
1771.	Mch. 21.	Josiah Edson appointed.[19]
		Winslow, Foster, Bradford, Edson.

SPECIAL JUSTICES COURT OF COMMON PLEAS.

1713.	Oct. 27.	Seth Arnold and Josiah Edson.
1727.	June 17.	Josiah Cotton.
1729.	Apr. 10.	Edward Winslow.
	Dec. 12.	Samuel Thaxter, Edward Winslow and Nicholas Sever.
1732.	Dec. 15.	Isaac Lothrop and Edward Winslow.
1740.	Oct. 27.	Thomas Croad.
1743.	Apr. 8.	John Little, Thomas Clap and Benjamin Stockbridge.
1751.	Apr. 24.	Thomas Foster.
1762.	Jan. 28.	Thomas Croade.
1763.	Feb. 17.	Josiah Edson and David Stockbridge.

SHERIFFS.

1692.	May 27.	John Bradford.
1699.	July 17.	James Warren.
1700.	June 7.	Capt. Seth Arnold.
1700–1.	Mch. 6.	Nathaniel Warren.
1702.	June 29.	Nathaniel Warren.
1706.	June 8.	Isaac Lothrop.
1715.	Dec. 9.	Isaac Lothrop.
1721.	Nov. 15.	Thomas Barker.
1728.	Dec. 12.	Thomas Barker.
1731.	Aug. 25.	{ Thomas Barker. John Holman.

[18] Bradford succeeded Cushing, who died June 26, 1762, aged 64.
[19] Edson took the place of Clapp, who probably resigned.

Sheriffs—Concluded.

DATE OF APPOINTMENT.	NAMES.
1733. June 22.	James Warren, (in place of Barker.)
1734. Apr. 23.	James Warren, (sole sheriff.)
1756. Sept. 14.	James Warren, Jr., (in place of Jas. Warren, resigned.)
1762. Jan. 28.	James Warren, Jr.

JUDGES AND REGISTERS OF PROBATE.

DATE OF APPOINTMENT.	JUDGES.	DATE OF APPOINTMENT.	REGISTERS.
1702. Aug. 13.	Nathaniel Thomas.	1700. June 7.	William Bassett.
1715. Dec. 9.	Nathaniel Thomas.	1702. Aug. 23.	Nathaniel Thomas, Jr.
1718. Nov. 20.	Isaac Winslow.	1715. Dec. 9.	Nathaniel Thomas, Jr.
1729. Aug. 22.	Isaac Winslow.	1729. Aug. 22.	Josiah Cotton.
1731. Aug. 25.	Isaac Winslow.	1731. Aug. 25.	Josiah Cotton.
1738–9. Jan. 12.	John Cushing.	1738–9. Jan. 12.	John Winslow.
1740. Oct. 27.	[Edward Winslow.]*	1762. Jan. 28.	Edward Winslow.
1746. Aug. 5.	John Cushing.		
1762. Jan. 28.	John Cushing.		

* During the absence of J. Cushing.

BRISTOL COUNTY.

INFERIOR COURT OF COMMON PLEAS.

DATE OF APPOINTMENT.		NAMES.
1692.	Dec. 7.	John Saffin, Thomas Leonard, Nicholas Peck and John Browne appointed.
		Saffin, Leonard, Peck, Browne.
1696.	Oct. 16.	The same confirmed.
1699.	July 17.	The same confirmed.
1701.	Aug. 7.	Nathaniel Byfield appointed.[1]
		Leonard, Peck, Browne, Byfield.
1702.	June 29.	Nathaniel Byfield, John Browne, Thomas Leonard and Ebenezer Brenton appointed.[2]
		Byfield, Browne, Leonard, Brenton.
1708.	Sept. 30.	Benjamin Church appointed.[3]
		Byfield, Browne, Leonard, Church.
1709.	Dec. 28.	Henry Mackintosh appointed.[4]
		Byfield, Leonard, Church, Mackintosh.
1710.	Aug. 24.	Nathaniel Payne appointed.[5]
		Leonard, Church, Mackintosh, Payne.
1713–14. Jan.	1.	Simon Davis appointed.[6]
		Church, Mackintosh, Payne, Davis.
1715.	Dec. 10.	Nathaniel Byfield, Nathaniel Payne, Henry Mackintosh and George Leonard appointed.[7]
		Byfield, Payne, Mackintosh, Leonard.

[1] Byfield took the place of John Saffin, transferred to the Superior Court.

Brenton took the place of Peck, who resigned, probably on account of age, being 80 years at his death, 27 May, 1710.

[3] Church filled the vacancy owing to the death of Ebenezer Brenton, who died

[4] Mackintosh succeeded John Browne, who died

[5] The cause of Payne's appointment was the following vote of the Council: "June 24, 1710. Upon consideration of the unmannerly and rude behaviour of Nathaniel Byfield, Esquire, yesterday to his Excellency the Governor and the Board, and his peremptory refusal to obey their order directed to him as Judge of Probate, *Advised*, That His Excellency be desired to suspend the said Nathaniel Byfield, Esquire, from the exercise of those civil offices that he holds under this Government."

[6] Davis succeeded Thomas Leonard, who died 24 Nov., 1713, aged 72.

[7] Byfield was re-appointed in place of Col. Church, who was old, as he died Jan. 17, 1717–18, aged 77. Leonard was in place of Davis.

Inferior Court of Common Pleas—Continued.

DATE OF APPOINTMENT.	NAMES.
1723–4. Mch. 19.	Nathaniel Blagrove appointed.[8]
	Byfield, Mackintosh, Payne, Blagrove.
1724. June 23.	Nathaniel Byfield, Henry Mackintosh, Seth Williams and Nathaniel Payne appointed.[9]
	Byfield, Mackintosh, Williams, Payne.
1724. Dec. 2.	Samuel Vyall appointed.[10]
	Payne, Mackintosh, Williams, Vyall.
1725. Dec. 18.	George Leonard appointed.[11]
	Payne, Williams, Vyall, Leonard.
1728. June 18.	Nathaniel Hubbard appointed.[12]
	Payne, Williams, Leonard, Hubbard.
1729. Aug. 22.	Nathaniel Payne, George Leonard, Nathaniel Hubbard, Thomas Church appointed.[13]
	Payne, Leonard, Hubbard, Church.
Dec. 12.	Seth Williams re-appointed.[14]
	Williams, Leonard, Hubbard, Church.
1733. June 22.	The same confirmed.
1740. Dec. 11.	Job Almy appointed.[15]
	Williams, Hubbard, Church, Almy.
1745–6. Feb. 8.	George Leonard and Stephen Payne appointed.[16]
	Williams, Almy, Leonard, Payne.
1747. June 27.	Ephraim Leonard appointed.[17]
	Williams, G. Leonard, Payne, E. Leonard.

[8] Blagrove was in the place of " Nathaniel Payne, deceased," says the Council Record, yet undoubtedly this was an error for George Leonard, who died 5 Sept., 1716. Payne is named until 1729.

[9] Williams succeeded Blagrove.

[10] Vyall was in the place of Byfield, " who has resigned."

[11] George Leonard, son of the former judge, probably took the place of Mackintosh.

[12] Hubbard succeeded Vyall, " who had resigned."

[13] Church took the place of Williams, who was omitted.

[14] Williams was re-appointed, " in the room of Nathaniel Payne, deceased."

[15] Almy was in the place of Leonard, who was left out for being concerned in the Land Bank, says Washburn, 369.

[16] Leonard, re-appointed, and Payne were " in the room of Nathaniel Hubbard and Thomas Church." Of these, Church was dead and Hubbard had been promoted to the Superior Court.

[17] Ephraim Leonard succeeded Almy.

Inferior Court of Common Pleas—Concluded.

DATE OF APPOINTMENT.		NAMES.
1749.	April 18.	Samuel Willis appointed.[18]
		Williams, G. Leonard, E. Leonard, Willis.
1760.	May 23.	George Leonard, Ephraim Leonard, Timothy Fales, James Williams appointed.[19]
		G. Leonard, E. Leonard, Fales, J. Williams.
1761.	Jan. 24.	Zepheniah Leonard appointed.[20]
		G. Leonard, E. Leonard, J. Williams, Z. Leonard.
	Nov. 24.	Same four confirmed.
1766.	June 18.	Elisha Tobey appointed.[21]
		G. Leonard, E. Leonard, J. Williams, Tobey.

SPECIAL JUSTICES COURT OF COMMON PLEAS.

1740.	Dec. 11.	Perez Bradford.
1735–6.	Jan. 9.	Job Almy and Jonathan Woodbury.
1745.	Apr. 5.	Nathaniel Hubbard.
1747.	June 27.	Thomas Terry and Samuel Willis.
1749.	Aug. 12.	Thomas Bowen and John Godfrey.
1761.	Jan. 24.	Samuel Willis.
	Nov. 24.	Samuel Willis and Thomas Bowen.
1763.	Feb. 17.	Thomas Gilbert.

SHERIFFS.

1692.	May 27.	Nathaniel Payne.
	Dec. 22.	Samuel Gallop, (in place of Payne, excused.)
1702.	June 29.	Samuel Gallop.
1710.	June 30.	Samuel Gallop.
1715.	Dec. 10.	William Troop.
1718.	Mch. 31.	Seth Williams, (coroner, to act in place of Gallop, deceased.)
	Apr. 16.	Charles Church.

[18] Willis was " in the room of Stephen Payne."

[19] Fales and J. Williams were in place of Seth Williams, who resigned and died May 13, 1764, aged 85, and Willis, who resigned and died Oct. 3, 1763, aged 79.

[20] Z. Leonard took the place of Fales, who resigned.

[21] Tobey succeeded Z. Leonard, who died 23 April, 1766.

Sheriffs—Concluded.

DATE OF APPOINTMENT.	NAMES.
1728. Dec. 12.	Charles Church.
1733. June 22.	Charles Church.
1746-7. Jan. 14.	Sylvester Richmond, Jr.
1761. Nov. 24.	Sylvester Richmond.

JUDGES AND REGISTERS OF PROBATE.

DATE OF APPOINTMENT.	JUDGES.	DATE OF APPOINTMENT.	REGISTERS.
1702. Oct. 23.	Nathaniel Byfield.	1702. Oct. 23.	John Carey.
1710. Aug. 24.	Nathaniel Payne.*	1715. Dec. 9.	Ebenezer Brenton.
1715. Dec. 9.	Nathaniel Byfield.	1721. July 20.	Stephen Payne.
1729. Sept. 27.	Nathaniel Blagrove.	1729. Sept. 27.	Stephen Payne.
1733. June 22.	Nathaniel Blagrove.	1733. June 22.	Stephen Payne.
1744. Apr. 5.	Nathaniel Hubbard.	1744. Apr. 5.	Stephen Payne.
1747-8. Feb. 16.	George Leonard.	1749. Apr. 18.	George Leonard, Jr.
1761. Nov. 24.	George Leonard.	1761. Nov. 24.	George Leonard, Jr.

* Byfield being suspended.

BARNSTABLE COUNTY.

COURT OF COMMON PLEAS.

DATE OF APPOINTMENT.		NAMES.
1692.	Dec. 7.	Barnabas Lothrop, John Freeman, John Thatcher and Stephen Skiffe appointed.
		Lothrop, Freeman, Thatcher, Skiffe.
1694–5.	Mch. 6.	Jonathan Sparrow appointed.[1]
		Lothrop, Thatcher, Skiffe, Sparrow.
1696.	Oct. 16.	Same four confirmed.
1699.	July 17.	Same four confirmed.
1702.	June 29.	Barnabas Lothrop, John Thatcher, Stephen Skiffe, John Otis appointed.[2]
		Lothrop, Thatcher, Skiffe, Otis.
1710.	June 22.	William Bassett appointed.[3]
		Lothrop, Thatcher, Otis, Bassett.
1711.	July 20.	John Gorham appointed.[4]
		Lothrop, Thatcher, Otis, Gorham.
1713.	June 5.	Daniel Parker.[5]
		Lothrop, Otis, Gorham, Parker.
1714.	June 15.	Thomas Paine appointed.[6]
		Lothrop, Otis, Parker, Paine.
1715.	Dec. 10.	John Otis, Daniel Parker, Thomas Paine, Nathaniel Freeman appointed.[7]
		Otis, Parker, Paine, Freeman.
1721.	Nov. 15.	Isaac Lothrop appointed.[8]
		Otis, Parker, Freeman, Lothrop.

[1] Sparrow was in the room of Freeman, resigned.
[2] John Otis succeeded Sparrow.
[3] Bassett succeeded Skiffe, who died
[4]
[5] Parker succeeded Col. John Thatcher, who died 8 May, 1713, aged 75.
[6]
[7] Freeman succeeded B. Lothrop, who died 1715.
[8] Lothrop succeeded "Thos. Paine, deceased."

Court of Common Pleas—Concluded.

DATE OF APPOINTMENT.	NAMES.
1727. Dec. 26.	Ezra Bourne appointed.[9]
	Parker, Freeman, I. Lothrop, Bourne.
1729. Apr. 10.	Peter Thatcher, Joseph Lothrop, Ezra Bourne and Shubael Baxter appointed.[10]
	Thatcher, Lothrop, Bourne, Baxter.
1731. Aug. 25.	The same confirmed.
1736. June 22.	John Thatcher appointed.[11]
	Lothrop, Bourne, Baxter, J. Thatcher.
1742–3. Jan. 27.	Shubael Gorham appointed[12]
	J. Thatcher, Gorham.
1746. Aug. 9.	John Otis appointed.[13]
1747–8. Mch. 1.	David Crocker appointed.[14]
1758. June 22.	John Thatcher, Sylvanus Bourne, David Crocker and Thomas Winslow appointed.[15]
	J. Thatcher, S. Bourne, Crocker, Winslow.
Aug. 3.	Thomas Smith, Jr., appointed.[16]
	Winslow, Smith.
1762. Jan. 21.	Sylvanus Bourne, Thomas Winslow, Thomas Smith and Edward Bacon appointed.[17]
	Bourne, Winslow, Smith, Bacon.
1764. Feb. 1.	James Otis appointed Chief Justice.[18]
	Otis, Winslow, Smith, Bacon.

[9] Bourne probably succeeded Otis, who died Nov. 30, 1727.

[10] Parker had died Dec. 23, 1728, aged 59; Freeman had probably resigned.

[11] John Thatcher undoubtedly succeeded his brother, Peter T., who died in 1735 or '6.

[12]

[13]

[14]

[15] Winslow succeeded John Otis, who died 4 May, 1758, and Bourne took the place made vacant, probably, by the resignation of

[16] Smith took the place of Crocker.

[17] Bourne was promoted to the place of Thatcher, who resigned, probably, and died Mch. 17, 1764, aged 89; Bacon filled the vacancy.

[18] Otis thus succeeded Bourne as Chief Justice, who died 18 Sept., 1763, aged 70.

SPECIAL JUSTICES COURT OF COMMON PLEAS.

DATE OF APPOINTMENT		NAMES.
1705.	Nov. 9.	Nathaniel Thomas and John Cushing.
1715.	July 14.	Samuel Sturgis and Meletiah Bourne.
1719.	June 27.	Samuel Sturgis and Nathaniel Freeman.
1721–2.	Mch. 16.	Josiah Edson and Jacob Thompson.
1722–3.	Jan. 9.	Joseph Doane and Meletiah Bourne.
1724.	Dec. 15.	Meletiah Bourne, Samuel Sturgis and Nathaniel Freeman.
1729.	April 10.	Nathaniel Freeman and Samuel Sturgis.
1730.	Dec. 24.	Same two; and again 1731, Sept. 1.
1736.	June 22.	John Doane and John Davis.
1739.	Dec. 21.	John Russell.
1742–3.	Jan. 27.	David Crocker.
1753.	Sept. 13.	Thomas Winslow.
1759.	Dec. 19.	Roland Robinson.
1762.	Jan. 21.	Roland Robinson.
1763.	Feb. 24.	Roland Cotton, and again April 7, 1763.
1765.	June 20.	John Gorham.
1770.	May 9.	Isaac Hinckley and Chillingworth Foster.

SHERIFFS.

1692.	May 25.	William Bassett.
1699.	July 17.	Samuel Allyn.
1702.	June 29.	Samuel Allyn.
1706.	June 8.	Jacob Thompson, (*pro hac vice.*)
1713–14. Jan.	1.	Shubael Gorham, (in place of S. Allyn, disabled by age.)
1715.	Dec. 10.	Joseph Lothrop.
1720.	July 22.	Shubael Gorham, (joint sheriff with Lothrop.)
1721.	Nov. 16.	John Russell.
1728.	Dec. 12.	Shubael Gorham.
1729.	Oct. 10.	John Russell, (jointly with Gorham.)

Sheriff's—Concluded.

DATE OF APPOINTMENT.	NAMES.	
1731.	Aug. 25.	Shubael Gorham and John Hedge, jointly.
1734-5.	Jan. 2.	Shubael Gorham, (sole sheriff.)
1740.	Oct. 27.	John Russell, (in place of Shubael Gorham, a member of the Council.)
1748.	Nov. 8.	John Gorham, (in place of John Russell, resigned.)
1762.	Jan. 21.	Joseph Otis.
1764.	Feb. 1.	Nathaniel Stone.

JUDGES AND REGISTERS OF PROBATE.

DATE OF APPOINTMENT.		JUDGES.	DATE OF APPOINTMENT.		REGISTERS.
1702.	Aug. 13.	Barnabas Lothrop.	1702.	Aug. 13.	William Bassett.
1714.	June 15.	John Otis.	1715.	Dec. 10.	William Bassett.
1715.	Dec. 10.	John Otis.	1721.	June 14.	Nathaniel Otis.
1727.	Dec. 26.	Meletiah Bourne.	1729.	Aug. 23.	Sylvanus Bourne.
1729.	Aug. 23.	Meletiah Bourne.	1731.	Aug. 25.	Sylvanus Bourne.
1731.	Aug. 25.	Meletiah Bourne.	1740-1.	Jan. 6.	David Gorham.
1740-1.	Jan. 6.	Sylvanus Bourne.	1762.	Jan. 21.	David Gorham.
1746.	Aug. 5.	Sylvanus Bourne.	1768.	Nov. 30.	David Gorham.
1762.	Jan. 21.	Sylvanus Bourne.			
1764.	Feb. 1.	James Otis.			

YORK COUNTY.

INFERIOR COURT OF COMMON PLEAS.

DATE OF APPOINTMENT.	NAMES.
1692. Dec. 7.	Job Alcock, Francis Hooke, Charles Frost and Samuel Wheelwright appointed.
	Alcock, Hooke, Frost, Wheelwright.
1694–5. Mch. 6.	William Pepperrell appointed.[1]
	Alcock, Frost, Wheelwright, Pepperrell.
1696. Oct. 10.	Samuel Wheelwright, Charles Frost, William Pepperrell and Samuel Donnell appointed.[2]
	Wheelwright, Frost, Pepperrell, Donnell.
1699. July 17.	Samuel Wheelwright, William Pepperrell and Samuel Donnell appointed.
Sept. 7.	Abraham Prebble appointed.[3]
	Wheelwright, Pepperrell, Donnell, Prebble.
1700. June 7.	Joseph Hammond appointed.[4]
	Pepperrell, Donnell, Prebble, Hammond.
1702. June 30.	Joseph Hammond, John Wheelwright, Ichabod Plaisted and Abraham Prebble appointed.[5]
	Hammond, Wheelwright, Plaisted, Prebble.
1708. June 15.	William Pepperrell appointed.[6]
	Hammond, Wheelwright, Plaisted, Pepperrell.
1710. June 8.	John Hill appointed.[7]
	Wheelwright, Plaisted, Pepperrell, Hill.

[1] Pepperrell was in the place of Francis Hooke, who died 10 Jan., 1694-5.

[2] Donnell took the place of Alcock.

[3] Prebble was in the place of Frost, who was killed by the Indians July 4, 1697.

[4] Hammond succeeded Samuel Wheelwright, who died 13 May, 1700.

[5] J. Wheelwright and Plaisted succeeded Pepperrell and Donnell, who were dropped, and Donnell lived till 1718.

[6] Pepperrell was in the place of Abraham Prebble, "disabled in his hearing," and who died 1 Oct., 1714, aged 72.

[7] Capt. J. Hill took the place of Joseph Hammond, who died 24 Feb., 1709-10.

Inferior Court of Common Pleas—Continued.

DATE OF APPOINTMENT.		NAMES.
1715.	Dec. 13.	John Wheelwright, William Pepperrell, Charles Frost and Abraham Prebble appointed.[8]
		Wheelwright, Pepperrell, Frost, Prebble.
1720.	Dec. 19.	Joseph Hammond appointed.[9]
		Wheelwright, Frost, Prebble, Hammond.
1724.	June 23.	Samuel Moody appointed.[10]
		Wheelwright, Frost, Hammond, Moody.
1724–5.	Feb. 18.	William Pepperrell, Jr., appointed.[11]
		Wheelwright, Hammond, Moody, Pepperrell.
1729.	April 11.	John Wheelwright, Joseph Hammond, William Pepperrell, Jr., and Samuel Came appointed.[12]
		Wheelwright, Hammond, Pepperrell, Came.
1731.	July 9.	William Pepperrell, Jr., Timothy Gerrish, Samuel Came and Joseph Moody appointed.[13]
		Pepperrell, Gerrish, Came, Moody.
1732.	Dec. 15.	Jeremiah Moulton appointed.[14]
		Pepperrell, Gerrish, Came, J. Moulton.
1739.	Oct. 5.	Elisha Gunnison appointed.[15]
		Pepperrell, Came, J. Moulton, Gunnison.
1749.	Aug. 12.	Simon Frost appointed.[16]
		Pepperrell, J. Moulton, Gunnison, Frost.
1753.	Jan. 2.	John Hill appointed.[17]
		Pepperrell, J. Moulton, Frost, Hill.

[8] Prebble, nephew of the former judge, and Charles Frost were appointed in room of Plaisted, who died 16 Nov., 1715, aged 54, and Hill.

[9] Hammond was in the place of William Pepperrell, "resigned."

[10] Moody succeeded Abraham Prebble, Jr., who died 14 Mch., 1723–4, aged 49.

[11] Pepperrell was in the room of Charles Frost, who died 17 Dec., 1724, aged 46.

[12] Came succeeded Moody, who lived till 1758.

[13] Gerrish and J. Moody succeeded Wheelwright and Hammond, who seem to have been dropped: W. lived till 1745 and H. till 1751.

[14] Moulton took the place of Joseph Moody, who "resigned to be a Justice of the Peace."

[15] Gunnison succeeded Timothy Gerrish, who "resigned."

[16] Frost was in the place of "Samuel Came, who had resigned."

[17] Hill succeeded Gunnison.

Inferior Court of Common Pleas—Concluded.

DATE OF APPOINTMENT.		NAMES.
1760.	May 23.	Jeremiah Moulton, Simon Frost, John Hill, Nathaniel Sparhawk appointed.[18]
		J. Moulton, Frost, Hill, Sparhawk.
1761.	Nov. 20.	Same four confirmed.
1765.	Sept. 11.	Joseph Sayer appointed.[19]
		J. Moulton, Hill, Sparhawk, Sayer.
1766.	Mch. 12.	Daniel Moulton appointed.[20]
		Hill, Sparhawk, Sayer, D. Moulton.
1772.	Mch. 18.	Nathaniel Sparhawk, Joseph Sayer, Daniel Moulton, James Gowen appointed.[21]
		Sparhawk, Sayer, Moulton, Gowen.
1774.	Apr. 7.	Jonathan Sayward appointed.[22]

SPECIAL JUSTICES COURT OF COMMON PLEAS.

1724–2.	Mch. 9.	Samuel Moody and Joseph Hill.
1725.	Sept. 30.	John Penhallow and Samuel Came.
1726.	Apr. 2.	Joseph Hill and Samuel Came.
1726.	June 18.	Joseph Hill and Samuel Came.
		John Gray and Samuel Came.
1726–7.	Feb. 23.	Joseph Hill and Samuel Came.
1727.	June 17.	Joseph Hill and Samuel Came.
	Dec. 22.	Joseph Hill and Samuel Came.
		Samuel Came and Nathaniel Gerrish.
	Dec. 26.	Samuel Came and Nathaniel Gerrish.
1728.	June 13.	Samuel Came and Nathaniel Gerrish.
1729.	Apr. 11.	Joseph Hill and Timothy Gerrish.
1730.	Dec. 24.	Joseph Hill and Timothy Gerrish.

---

[18] Sparhawk filled the vacancy left by Pepperell's death, July 6, 1759.
[19] Sayer succeeded Moulton, who died 20 July, 1765.
[20] D. Moulton succeeded Frost, who died   1766. Hill was made first justice at the same date.
[21] Gowen succeeded John Hill, who died 2 Mch., 1772.
[22] Sayward

Special Justices Court of Common Pleas—Concluded.

DATE OF APPOINTMENT.	NAMES.
1731–2. Mch. 21.	John Gray and Joshua Moody.
1733. Oct. 26.	John Hill and Elihu Gunnison.
1733–4. Feb. 14.	John Hill, Elihu Gunnison and Joseph Hill.
1734. Dec. 27.	Joshua Moody, Thomas Smith and Joseph Sawyer.
1738–9. Jan. 12.	Peter Nowell.
1743. Apr. 8.	John Hill, Joseph Sawyer and John Storer.
1744–5. Mch. 21.	John Hill and Joshua Moody.
1747. June 27.	John Hill and Richard Cutts, Jr.
1749. Apr. 18.	John Storer.
1751. June 21.	John Storer.
1755. June 26.	Joseph Sayer and Charles Frost.
1761. Nov. 20.	Joseph Sayer, Richard Cutt, John Storer and Daniel Moulton.
1772. Mch. 18.	Jonathan Sayward.

SHERIFFS.

1692.	May 27.	Joseph Hammond, (who declined.)
	Dec. 8.	Jonathan Hammond.
1702.	June 30.	Joseph Curtis.
1706.	Nov. 8.	Charles Frost.
1713.	Oct. 27.	Abraham Prebble, Jr.
1715.	Dec. 13.	John Leighton.
1724.	Dec. 2.	Jeremiah Moulton.
1728.	Dec. 12.	Jeremiah Moulton.
1731.	July 9.	Jeremiah Moulton.
1752.	Sept. 19.	Jeremiah Moulton, Jr.
1759.	Dec. 19.	Jeremiah Moulton, Jr.
1761.	Nov. 20.	Jeremiah Moulton, Jr.
1771.	Apr. 12.	Jotham Moulton.

JUDGES AND REGISTERS OF PROBATE.

Date of Appointment.	JUDGES.	Date of Appointment.	REGISTERS.
1694–5. Mch. 6.	Samuel Wheelwright.	1694. Dec. 4.	Joseph Hammond.*
1700. June 7.	Joseph Hammond.	1700. June 7.	Charles Frost.
1702. Aug. 13.	Joseph Hammond.	1702. Aug. 13.	Charles Frost.
1710. June 8.	Ichabod Plaisted.	1715. Dec. 13.	Charles Frost.
1715. Dec. 13.	John Wheelwright.	1724–5. Feb. 18.	Charles Frost.
1729. Aug. 23.	John Wheelwright.	1729. Aug. 23.	Charles Frost.
1731. July 9.	John Wheelwright.	1731. July 9.	Charles Frost.
1745. Dec. 20.	Jeremiah Moulton.	1733. Oct. 26.	Robert Eliot Gerrish.
1761. Nov. 20.	Jeremiah Moulton.	1744. Nov. 1.	Simon Frost.
1765. Sept. 11.	John Hill.	1761. Nov. 20.	Simon Frost.
1772. Mch. 18.	Jonathan Sayward.	1766. Mch. 12.	David Sewall.

* Hammond was also Clerk of the Court of Common Pleas and Register of Deeds, succeeding Capt. John Wincoll, deceased.

NANTUCKET COUNTY.

COURT OF COMMON PLEAS.

DATE OF APPOINTMENT.		NAMES.
1696.	Oct. 16.	John Gardner, James Coffin, William Geare, William Worth appointed.
		J. Gardner, Coffin, Geare, Worth.
1699.	July 17.	John Gardner, James Coffin, William Worth appointed.[1]
		J. Gardner, Coffin, Worth.
	Sept. 7.	William Geare appointed.
		J. Gardner, Coffin, Worth, Geare.
1702.	June 29.	Same four confirmed.
1706.	June 6.	Richard Gardner appointed.[2]
		Coffin, Worth, Geare, R. Gardner.
1711.	June 8.	George Gardner appointed.[3]
		Coffin, Worth, R. Gardner, G. Gardner.
1715.	Dec. 13.	James Coffin, William Worth, Richard Gardner, George Bunker appointed.[4]
		Jas. Coffin, Worth, R. Gardner, Bunker.
1718.	June 27.	George Gardner, Joseph Coffin appointed.[5]
		R. Gardner, Bunker, G. Gardner, Coffin.
1719.	Nov. 25.	John Coffin appointed.[6]
		R. Gardner, Bunker, G. Gardner, Jno. Coffin.
1728.	June 28.	Joseph Gardner appointed.[7]
		Bunker, G. Gardner, Jno. Coffin, J. Gardner.

[1] Only three judges then appointed, objection being made to Geare.
[2] Richard Gardner succeeded John Gardner, "lately deceased," who died May 6, 1706, aged 82.
[3] George Gardner took the place of Geare, who died 23 Sept., 1710.
[4] George Bunker took the place of George Gardner, who probably resigned, as he did not die till 17 Apr., 1750.
[5] James Coffin probably resigned, and died 8 July, 1720. Worth was superseded or resigned, and died Dec., 1724.
[6] John Coffin took the place of Joseph Coffin, who died 15 July, 1719.
[7] Joseph Gardner succeeded Richard Gardner, who died May 8, 1728.

Court of Common Pleas—Concluded.

DATE OF APPOINTMENT.		NAMES.
1729.	Oct. 10.	George Bunker, George Gardner, John Coffin, Joseph Gardner appointed.[8]
		Bunker, G. Gardner, Jno. Coffin, J. Gardner.
1732.	July 6.	Same four confirmed.
1744.	Dec. 21.	Josiah Coffin appointed.[9]
1744–5.	Jan. 3.	Thomas Brock appointed.[9]
		G. Gardner, Jno. Coffin, Josiah Coffin, Brock.
1747.	Sept. 11.	Josiah Coffin, Thomas Brock, Jonathan Coffin and Grafton Gardner appointed.[10]
		Josiah Coffin, Brock, Jona. Coffin, Gr. Gardner.
1751.	June 21.	John Bunker appointed.[11]
		Jos. Coffin, Jona. Coffin, Gr. Gardner, J. Bunker.
1761.	Nov. 20.	Josiah Coffin, Jonathan Coffin, Grafton Gardner and Caleb Bunker appointed.[12]
		Josiah Coffin, Jona. Coffin, Gr. Gardner, C. Bunker.
1767.	Nov. 4.	Obed Hussey appointed.[13]
		Josiah Coffin, Grafton Gardner, C. Bunker, Hussey.

SPECIAL JUSTICES COURT OF COMMON PLEAS.

1712.	Oct. 24.	Ephraim Hunt, Isaac Winslow, John Cushing and Samuel Thaxter.
1727–8.	Jan. 24.	Capt. Ebenezer Coffin.
1739.	June 22.	Joseph Lothrop, Ezra Bourne, Shubal Baxter and John Thatcher.
1742.	July 8.	John Cushing, Zaccheus Mayhew, Silvanus Bourne and Enoch Coffin.

[8] A confirmation of the existing bench.
[9] Josiah Coffin succeeded George Bunker, who died 24 Nov., 1744, and Brock was "in the room of Joseph Gardner, Esq.;" Gardner died 29 Sept., 1747.
[10] George Gardner was superseded or resigned, and died 17 Apr., 1750; John Coffin died 1 Sept., 1747. There were thus two vacancies, filled by Jona. Coffin and Grafton Gardner.
[11] John Bunker took the place of Brock.
[12] Caleb Bunker was appointed Nov. 12, 1761, succeeding John Bunker, who died 1 Nov., 1760.
[13] Obed Hussey succeeded

SHERIFFS

DATE OF APPOINTMENT.	NAMES.
1702. June 30.	Jethro Coffin.
1707. Apr. 15.	John Coffin.
1715. Dec. 13.	John Coffin, (Marshal.)
1719. Nov. 25.	Samuel Coffin.
1720. July 22.	John Coffin, Jr.
1729. Oct. 10.	John Coffin, Jr.
1732. July 6.	John Coffin, Jr.
1747. Sept. 11.	John Coffin, Jr.
1760. May 23.	Benjamin Tupper.
1761. Nov. 20.	Benjamin Tupper.

JUDGES AND REGISTERS OF PROBATE.

DATE OF APPOINTMENT.	JUDGES.	DATE OF APPOINTMENT.	REGISTERS.
	John Gardner.	1715. Dec. 13.	George Gardner.
1706. June 6.	James Coffin.*	1732. July 6.	Eleazer Folger.
1715. Dec. 13.	James Coffin.	1747. Sept. 11.	Eleazer Folger.
1728. June 28.	George Bunker.	1754. Jan. 16.	Frederick Folger.
1732. July 6.	George Gardner.	1761. Nov. 20.	Frederick Folger.
1744. Dec. 21.	George Gardner.		
1747. Sept. 11.	Jeremiah Gardner.		
1761. Nov. 20.	Jeremiah Gardner.		
1767. Mch. 25.	Grafton Gardner.		

* Coffin succeeded Gardner, but I do not find the appointment of this latter.

DUKES COUNTY.

COURT OF COMMON PLEAS.

DATE OF APPOINTMENT.	NAMES.
1692. Dec. 7.	Matthew Mayhew, Thomas Mayhew and James Allin appointed.
	M. Mayhew, T. Mayhew, Allin.
1696. Oct. 16.	Matthew Mayhew, Thomas Mayhew, James Allin, John Coffin appointed.
	M. Mayhew, T. Mayhew, Allin, Coffin.
1699. July 17.	Thomas Mayhew, James Allin, John Coffin appointed.[1]
	T. Mayhew, Allin, Coffin.
Sept. 6.	Benjamin Skiffe appointed.
	T. Mayhew, Allin, Coffin, Skiffe.
1702. June 29.	Thomas Mayhew, James Allin, Benjamin Skiffe, Joseph Norton appointed.[2]
	T. Mayhew, Allin, Skiffe, Norton.
1713. Oct. 27.	Paine Mayhew appointed.[3]
	Allin, Skiffe, Norton, P. Mayhew.
1715. Dec. 10.	Benjamin Skiffe, Paine Mayhew, Joseph Norton, Ebenezer Allen appointed.[4]
	Skiffe, P. Mayhew, J. Norton, E. Allen.
1718. Apr. 16.	Zaccheus Mayhew appointed.[5]
	P. Mayhew, J. Norton, E. Allen, Z. Mayhew.
1722. June 29.	John Chipman appointed.[6]
	P. Mayhew, E. Allen, Z. Mayhew, Chipman.
1727–8. Jan. 24.	Enoch Coffin appointed.[7]
	P. Mayhew, E. Allen, Z. Mayhew, Coffin.

[1] Only three judges appointed; Matthew Mayhew was probably the teacher of the Indians, and resigned.
[2] Norton took the place of Coffin, who lived, however, till 5 Sept., 1711.
[3] Paine Mayhew succeeded Thomas Mayhew, probably, who died 21 July, 1715.
[4] Allen succeeded James Allin, his father, who died 25 July, 1714, aged 77.
[5] Zaccheus Mayhew succeeded Skiffe, who died 18 Feb., 1718.
[6] John Chipman was "in the place of John Norton," says the Council record, an error, doubtless, for Joseph Norton, who lived till 30 Jan., 1741.
[7] E. Coffin succeeded J. Chipman.

Court of Common Pleas—Concluded.

DATE OF APPOINTMENT.		NAMES.
1729.	Oct. 10.	Paine Mayhew, Ebenezer Allen, Zaccheus Mayhew, Enoch Coffin appointed.[8]
		P. Mayhew, E. Allen, Z. Mayhew, Coffin.
1733.	May 4.	Zaccheus Mayhew, Enoch Coffin, John Allen, Samuel Norton appointed.[9]
		Z. Mayhew, Coffin, J. Allen, S. Norton.
1748.	Apr. 15.	Zaccheus Mayhew, Enoch Coffin, John Allen, John Sumner appointed.[10]
		Z. Mayhew, Coffin, Allen, Sumner.
1761.	Jan. 24.	Ebenezer Smith appointed.[11]
		Coffin, Allen, Sumner, Smith.
	Oct. 16.	John Allen, John Sumner, Ebenezer Smith, John Newman appointed.[12]
		Allen, Sumner, Smith, Newman.
1762.	Jan. 21.	Matthew Mayhew, first justice, appointed.[13]
		M. Mayhew, Sumner, Smith, Newman.
1764.	June 8.	Josiah Tilton appointed.[14]
		M. Mayhew, Sumner, Smith, Tilton.
1771.	Dec. 10.	Joseph Mayhew appointed.[15]
		M. Mayhew, Sumner, Tilton, J. Mayhew.
		To the Revolution.

SPECIAL JUSTICES COURT OF COMMON PLEAS.

1730.	Dec. 24.	John Worth and Benjamin Smith.
1732.	July 6.	Joseph Lothrop and John Thatcher.
	July 7.	Joseph Lothrop and John Thatcher.

[8] This was a confirmation of the existing bench.

[9] John Allen and Samuel Norton took the places of Ebenezer Allen, who died 14 May, 1733, and Paine Mayhew, who lived till 8 May, 1761.

[10] Sumner succeeded Norton, who did not die till 16 Feb., 1760.

[11] Ebenezer Smith filled the vacancy at the death of Z. Mayhew, 3 Jan., 1760, aged 75.

[12] Newman was in the place of Enoch Coffin, who died in 1761.

[13] Matthew Mayhew was appointed as first justice, in place of John Allen, probably superseded, as he died, aged 84, 17 Oct., 1767.

[14] Tilton took the place of Newman, who died 1 Dec., 1763.

[15] Joseph Mayhew succeeded Smith, who died 15 Oct., 1771, aged 71.

Special Justices Court of Common Pleas—Concluded.

Date of Appointment.	Names.
1733–4. Feb. 21.	Benjamin Smith and Ebenezer Norton.
1741–2. Jan. 15.	Jabez Athearn and Samuel Basset.
1757. Aug. 26.	Ebenezer Norton, in the cause of Ann, widow of John Allen, Jr., in room of Zaccheus Mayhew and John Allen, related to said Ann.
1761. Oct. 16.	Josiah Tilton.
1771. Dec. 10.	John Worth.

[Note.—The court records are very imperfect. Richard Sarson was a justice of the peace before 1692, and certainly until 1697. He seems to have acted as a special justice in this court.]

SHERIFFS.

Date of Appointment.	Names.	Date of Appointment.	Names.
1701. June 12.	Ebenezer Allin.	1733. May 4.	Eleazer Allen.
1702. June 29.	Ebenezer Allin.	1735–6. Jan. 2.	Thomas Mayhew.
1715. Sept. 16.	John Allen.	1743. Oct. 20.	John Norton.
Dec. 10.	John Allen.	1761. Oct. 16.	John Norton.
1728. Dec. 12.	John Allen.	1772. Apr. 23.	William Mayhew.

JUDGES AND REGISTERS OF PROBATE.

Date of Appointment.	Judges.	Date of Appointment.	Registers.
1696. Oct. 16.	Matthew Mayhew.	1696. Oct. 16.	Matthew Mayhew, Jr.
1710. June 22.	Benjamin Skiffe.	1715. Dec. 10.	Matthew Mayhew.
1715. Dec. 10.	Benjamin Skiffe.	1718. Apr. 16.	Jabez Athearn.
1718. Apr. 16.	Paine Mayhew.	1729. Sept. 27.	Jabez Athearn.
1729. Sept. 27.	Paine Mayhew.	1733. May 4.	Jabez Athearn.
1733. May 4.	Zaccheus Mayhew.	1748. Apr. 15.	Jabez Athearn.
1748. Apr. 15.	Zaccheus Mayhew.	1761. Oct. 16.	Jabez Athearn.
1760. May 23.	Matthew Mayhew.	Nov. 20.	James Athearn.
1761. Oct. 16.	Matthew Mayhew.		

WORCESTER COUNTY.

COURT OF COMMON PLEAS.

DATE OF APPOINTMENT.	NAMES.
1731. June 30.	John Chandler, Joseph Wilder, William Ward, William Jennison appointed. *Chandler, Wilder, Ward, Jennison.*
1739. Oct. 5.	Joseph Dwight appointed.[1] *Wilder, Ward, Jennison, Dwight.*
1742–3. Jan. 27.	Samuel Willard appointed.[2] *Wilder, Ward, Dwight, Willard.*
1744. Dec. 21.	Nahum Ward appointed.[3] *Wilder, Dwight, Willard, N. Ward.*
1750. Mch. 29.	Edward Hartwell appointed.[4] *Wilder, Dwight or Hartwell, Willard, Ward.*
1753. Jan. 2.	Edward Hartwell appointed.[5] *Wilder, Dwight, Ward, Hartwell.*
1754. Apr. 19.	John Chandler appointed.[6] *Wilder, Ward, Hartwell, Chandler.*
1755. June 26.	Thomas Steel appointed.[7] *Wilder, Hartwell, Chandler, Steel.*
1757. Apr. 19.	John Chandler, Edward Hartwell, Thomas Steel and Timothy Ruggles appointed.[8] *Chandler, Hartwell, Steel, Ruggles.*
1762. Jan. 21.	Timothy Ruggles, Thomas Steel, Joseph Wilder and Artemas Ward appointed.[9] *Ruggles, Steel, Wilder, Ward.[10]*

[1] Joseph Dwight was "in the room of John Chandler, Esq., who has resigned."

[2] Willard succeeded Jennison, who died 19 Sept., 1741.

[3] Nahum Ward was "in the room of William Ward."

[4] Hartwell's first appointment was "in the room of Joseph Dwight, Esq'. and during his sickness." Dwight was then in the army.

[5] Hartwell was again appointed, succeeding Willard, who died   Nov., 1752, aged 62.

[6] Chandler succeeded, as Dwight had been transferred to Hampshire, 4th Jan., 1753; it is *possible* that during this time Jonas Rice had been commissioned, and he died 22 Sept., 1754, aged 84, but there is no record of his being other than a special justice, acting during a vacancy.

[7] Steel succeeded N. Ward, who died 7 May, 1754, aged 70.

[8] Ruggles filled the vacancy caused by the death of Wilder, 29 Mch., 1757, aged 74.

[9] A. Ward and J. Wilder (son of the former judge,) succeeded John Chandler, who died 1763, aged 70, and Edward Hartwell, who died 17 Feb., 1785, aged 96.

[10] Wilder died Apr. 29, 1775, aged 65, but no successor appears to have been named before the Revolution.

SPECIAL JUSTICES COURT OF COMMON PLEAS.

DATE OF APPOINTMENT.	NAMES.
1733–4. Feb. 21.	Joseph Dwight and Nahum Ward.
1743. June 23.	Nahum Ward and Edward Hartwell.
1745. Apr. 5.	Edward Hartwell.
Apr. 26.	James Rice.
1749–50. Mch. 29.	Jonas Rice.
1753. Jan. 2.	Jonas Rice.
1754. Jan. 16.	Thomas Steel and Joseph Wilder, Jr.
1755. June 26.	Samuel Willard and Artemas Ward.
1762. Jan. 21.	John Murray.

SHERIFFS.

1731. June 30.	Daniel Gookin.
1743. June 23.	Benjamin Flagg.
1751. June 21.	John Chandler, Jr.
1762. Jan. 21.	John Chandler, Jr.
Aug. 12.	Gardner Chandler.

JUDGES AND REGISTERS OF PROBATE.

DATE OF APPOINTMENT.	JUDGES.	DATE OF APPOINTMENT.	REGISTERS.
1731. June 30.	John Chandler.	1731. June 30.	John Chandler, Jr.
1739. Oct. 5.	Joseph Wilder.	1746. Oct. 8.	John Chandler.
1746. Aug. 5.	Joseph Wilder.	1757. Apr. 19.	Timothy Paine.
1757. Apr. 19.	John Chandler.	1762. Jan. 21.	Timothy Paine.
1762. Jan. 21.	John Chandler.	1766. Aug. 6.	{ Timothy Paine.*
Aug. 12.	John Chandler.		{ Clark Chandler.*

* Jointly.

LINCOLN COUNTY.

COURT OF COMMON PLEAS.

DATE OF APPOINTMENT.		NAMES.
1760.	Oct. 31.	Samuel Dennie, William Lithgow, Aaron Hinckley, John North appointed.
		Dennie, Lithgow, Hinckley, North.
1761.	Oct. 16.	Same four confirmed.
1763.	Sept. 7.	Thomas Rice appointed.[1]
1771.	Nov. 4.	Thomas Goldthwaite appointed.[2]

SPECIAL JUSTICES COURT OF COMMON PLEAS.

1763.	Sept. 7.	James Howard.
1764.	July 18.	Samuel Danforth, Nathaniel Ropes, Timothy Ruggles and Samuel White.
	Aug. 25.	Thomas Goldthwaite, Alexander Ross and Solomon Lombard.
1767.	Aug. 5.	Thomas Goldthwaite.
1774.	Feb. 7.	James McCobb.

SHERIFFS.

1760.	Oct. 31.	Charles Cushing.
1761.	Oct. 16.	Charles Cushing.

JUDGES AND REGISTERS OF PROBATE.

DATE OF APPOINTMENT.		JUDGES.	DATE OF APPOINTMENT.		REGISTERS.
1760.	Oct. 31.	William Cushing.	1760.	Oct. 31.	William Bryant.
1761.	Oct. 16.	William Cushing.	1761.	Jan. 24.	Jonathan Bowman.
1772.	Mch. 4.	Jonathan Bowman.		Oct. 16.	Jonathan Bowman.[3]
			1772.	June 17.	Rowland Cushing.

[1] Rice succeeded   [2] Hartwell succeeded   [3] Also Commissioner, as Register of Deeds.

CUMBERLAND COUNTY.

COURT OF COMMON PLEAS.

DATE OF APPOINTMENT.		NAMES.
1760.	Nov. 13.	John Minot, Ezekiel Cushing, Enoch Freeman and Edward Milliken appointed.
		Minot, Cushing, Freeman, Milliken.
1761.	Oct. 16.	Same appointed.
1763.	Feb. 24.	Jeremiah Powell, Ezekiel Cushing, Enoch Freeman, Edward Milliken appointed.[1]
		Powell, Cushing, Freeman, Milliken.
1765.	July 3.	Alexander Ross appointed.[2]
		Powell, Freeman, Milliken, Ross.
1769.	Aug. 3.	Moses Pearson appointed.[3]
		Powell, Freeman, Milliken, Pearson.
1772.	June 17.	Jeremiah Powell, Enoch Freeman, Moses Pearson, Jonas Mason appointed.[4]
		Powell, Freeman, Pearson, Mason.

SPECIAL JUSTICES COURT OF COMMON PLEAS.

1761.	Oct. 16.	Alexander Ross.
1762.	Apr. 21.	Jeremiah Powell.
1764.	Mch. 7.	Jonas Mason.
1765.	July 3.	Solomon Lombard.
	Aug. 7.	Jonas Mason.
1768.	Feb. 24.	Moses Pearson.

[1] Powell was appointed first justice, in the place of Minot.
[2] Ross took the place of Cushing, who died in 1765.
[3] Pearson succeeded Ross, who died 24 Nov., 1768.
[4] Mason was in the place of Milliken.

SHERIFFS.

DATE OF APPOINTMENT.	NAMES.
1760. Oct. 31.	Moses Pearson.
1761. Oct. 16.	Moses Pearson.
1767. Dec. 2.	William Tyng.

JUDGES AND REGISTERS OF PROBATE.

DATE OF APPOINTMENT.	JUDGES.	DATE OF APPOINTMENT.	REGISTERS.
1760. Oct. 31.	Samuel Waldo.	1760. Oct. 31.	Joseph Stockbridge.
1761. Oct. 16.	Samuel Waldo.	1761. Oct. 16.	Stephen Longfellow.
1770. May 9.	Enoch Freeman.		

BERKSHIRE COUNTY.

COURT OF COMMON PLEAS.

DATE OF APPOINTMENT.	NAMES.
1761. June 24.	Joseph Dwight, William Williams, John Ashley, Timothy Woodbridge appointed.
	Dwight, Williams, Ashley, Woodbridge.
1765. Sept. 6.	Perez Marsh appointed.[1]
	Williams, Ashley, Woodbridge, Marsh.

SPECIAL JUSTICES COURT OF COMMON PLEAS.

DATE OF APPOINTMENT.	NAMES.	DATE OF APPOINTMENT.	NAMES.
1765. June 6.	Perez Marsh.	1765. Sept. 6.	Elijah Dwight.

SHERIFFS.

1761. June 24.	Elijah Williams.	1774. Feb. 18.	Israel Stoddard.

JUDGES AND REGISTERS OF PROBATE.

DATE OF APPOINTMENT.	JUDGES.	DATE OF APPOINTMENT.	REGISTERS.
1761. June 24.	Josiah Dwight.	1761. June 24.	Elijah Dwight.
1765. Sept. 6.	William Williams.		

[1] Perez Marsh succeeded Joseph Dwight, who had held the post in Worcester, Hampshire and Berkshire and died June 9, 1765, aged 62.

ATTORNEY-GENERAL.

Date of Appointment.	Names.	Date of Appointment.	Names.
1692. Oct. 28.	Anthony Checkley.[1]	1733. June 21.	John Read.[7]
1702. July 6.	Paul Dudley.[2]	1736. June 22.	William Brattle.[8]
1718.		1738.	
1719.		1739.	
1720. July 19.	Thomas Newton.[3]	1740. July 2.	John Overing.[9]
1722. June	John Overing.[4]	1742.	Jeremiah Gridley.[10]
1723. June 20.	John Read.[5]	1743.	John Overing.[11]
1724. June 12.	John Read.	1747. June 24.	William Brattle[12]
1725. June 15.	John Read.	1748. June 24.	James Otis.[13]
1726. June 21.	John Read.	1749. June 29.	Edmund Trowbridge.[14]
1727. June 28.	John Read.	1767. Mch. 25.	Jeremiah Gridley.[15]
1728.	John Overing.[6]	Nov. 18.	Jonathan Sewall.[16]

[1] Anthony Checkley appointed by the Governor and Council.

[2] Dudley was appointed Nov. 20th, 1715. The House elected Thomas Newton, but the Council did not concur. June 8th, 1716, Dudley was elected, and again June 19, 1717, the Governor having yielded his claim to nominate. In April, 1718, Dudley was appointed Judge of the Superior Court, and probably resigned this office.

[3] Newton was elected in 1720 and probably in 1721, as Washburn says he was in office at his death, 28th May, 1721.

[4] Overing was elected by the House.

[5] Read was elected for five successive years by the House.

[6] John Overing was commissioned by the Governor and Council. June 12th, 1728, the House chose Addington Davenport, Jr., but this was of no effect. In 1731, Jan. 5th, the House chose John Read, and July 4th, 1732, the House chose Addington Davenport, Jr., but the Governor resisted in both cases.

[7] Read was elected by the House, the Governor having yielded, and he was re-elected 15th June, 1733, and June 18th, 1735.

[8] Brattle was elected by the House, and again 5th July, 1737.

[9] Overing was elected this year, and also 31st July, 1741.

[10] Gridley was in office for one year, says Washburn.

[11] Washburn says Overing was re-elected annually for several years.

[12] Brattle was elected by the House.

[13] Otis was elected by the House, and again 22d June, 1749; yet this last election was probably void.

[14] Trowbridge was commissioned by the Governor and Council. He was also chosen June 30, 1750, by the House, but the controversy then ended, and he continued to act under his commission until his appointment to the Superior Court in 1767.

[15] Gridley was appointed with Jonathan Sewall to be Special Attorney-General in all cases where Gridley should be prevented attending. Gridley died 7 Sept., 1767.

[16] Sewall was appointed by the Governor and Council, and held office till the Revolution.

SOLICITOR-GENERAL.

DATE OF APPOINTMENT.	NAMES.
1767. June 24.	Jonathan Sewall.[1]
1771. Mch. 21.	Samuel Quincy.

[1] This office was created for Sewall, who, however, was made Attorney-General 18 Nov. of the same year. Washburn says that Quincy succeeded in the office, though there is no record of his appointment until 1771, as above noted.

COMMISSIONERS OF IMPOST AND EXCISE.

(ELECTED ANNUALLY.)

DATE OF APPOINTMENT.	NAMES.
1692. June 24.	Elisha Hutchinson, Jonathan Corwin and John Walley.
1693. April 6.	Elisha Hutchinson and John Walley.
1694. June 8.	John Walley.
1695.	John Walley.
1696. June 17.	James Tailer.
1697. June 18.	John Walley.
June 19.	John Walley, Nathaniel Byfield and Maj. Converse.
1698. June 27.	John Walley and Elisha Hutchinson.
1699. July 25.	John Walley and Penn Townsend.
Aug. 24.	William Payne.
1704. June 28.	James Russell.[1]
1709. April 30.	Elisha Hutchinson.[2]
June 10.	Daniel Russell.[3]
1762. Feb. 5.	James Russell.[4]

[1] James Russell held for several years, though the record seems imperfect.

[2] Hutchinson was appointed to fill the vacancy at Russell's death.

[3] Daniel Russell, son of James, seems to have been elected almost every year, and was doubtless in continuous service.

[4] James Russell was elected yearly until 1774.

JUSTICES OF THE PEACE.

[Those marked with a * were also of the Quorum.]

SUFFOLK.

1692.	May 27.	Dean Winthrop.
		Eliakim Hutchinson.*
		Capt. Penn Townsend.*
		Nathaniel Oliver.
		Edward Bromfield.
		Capt. Ephraim Hunt.
		Capt. Timothy Prout.
		Jeremiah Dummer.*
		John Eyre.
		Capt. John Smith.
		Major Edmund Quincy.*
		Daniel Cushing.
		Capt. Timothy Dwight.
1700.	June 7.	James Bailey.
		John Wilson.
		John Clark.
1701.	June 12.	Major Samuel Eells.
1702.	June 30.	Jeremiah Dummer.
		Edward Bromfield.
		Charles Hobby.
		Thomas Brattle.
		Nathaniel Oliver.
		Nicholas Paige.
		Jahleel Brenton.[1]
		Samuel Legg.
		Paul Dudley.
		John Nelson.
		Ephraim Hunt.
		John Clarke.
		Thomas Palmer.
		Samuel Eells.
		James Bailey.
		Edward Lyde.
		William Tailer.
		Adam Winthrop.
		John Wilson.
	Nov. 19.	Samuel Lynde.
1706.	June 18.	Simeon Stoddard.
		Capt. Thos. Hutchinson.

1706.	June 18.	Edmund Quincy.
		William Clarke.
		Samuel Sewall, Jr.
1707.	June 5.	Capt. John Chandler.[2]
1708-9.	Feb. 25.	Addington Davenport.[3]
1709.	June 23.	Major Samuel Thaxter.
1713.	Aug. 12.	Nathaniel Hubbard.
		William Dudley.
	Oct. 27.	Col. Samuel Checkley.
1715.	Apr. 7.	Major Thomas Fitch.
	Dec. 9.	Jeremiah Dummer.
		Nicholas Paige.
		Samuel Lynde.
		Thomas Palmer.
		Edward Lyde.
		Josiah Chapin.
		Simeon Stoddard.
		John Nelson.
		Samuel Thaxter.
		John Chandler.
		Samuel Checkley.
		Nathaniel Hubbard.
		William Harris.
		David Jeffries.
		Elisha Cooke.
		Edward Hutchinson.
		William Dennison.
		Robert Spur.
		John Quincy.
	Dec. 10.	Oliver Noyes.
		Anthony Stoddard.
		Grove Hirst.
		William Hutchinson.
		Elisha Danforth.
	Dec. 24.	Thomas Newton.
		Samuel Keeling.
1717.	Nov. 12.	John Nelson.
		Elijah Danforth.
1718.	Apr. 16.	John Valentine.

[1] Rejected. [2] Of Woodstock. [3] John Wilson to be left out.

Justices of the Peace—Continued.

1718.	Nov. 20.	Edward Lynde.	1728.	Dec. 19.	William Pepperrell.
1719.	June 27.	Jeremiah Allen.			Josiah Willard.
1721.	Nov. 15.	Thomas Steel.			Samuel Sewall.
		John White.			Edward Bromfield.
1722-3.	Jan. 9.	Samuel Sewall, Jr.			Thomas Palmer.
		Joseph White.			Edward Hutchinson.
	Mch. 20.	Thomas Lechmere.			Samuel Checkley.
		John Ruck.			John Nelson.
1723.	Sept. 6.	John Campbell.			William Dudley.
1723-4.	Mch. 4.	John Alford.			Samuel Sewall, Jr.
1724-5.	Feb. 18.	Joseph Wadsworth.			Anthony Stoddard.
		Joshua Lamb.			Timothy Clerk.
		Robert Spur.			Habijah Savage.
	Feb. 19.	John Ballantine.			Elijah Danforth.
1725.	Sept. 2.	Stephen Minot.			Thomas Steel.
1726.	June 2.	Nathaniel Green.			Thomas Lechmere.
1727.	Dec. 26.	Jonathan Ware.[1]			John Ruck.
1728.	June 18.	Edward Hutchinson.[*]			Joseph Wadsworth.
		Anthony Stoddard.			Joshua Lamb.
		Major John Bolls.			Robert Spurr.
	June 19.	Habijah Savage.			John Ballantine.
	Dec. 19.	Elijah Danforth.[2]			Stephen Minot.
		Hon. William Dummer.			Nathaniel Green.
		William Tailer.			John Bowles.
		Nathaniel Byfield.			Jonathan Ware.
		Isaac Window.			Francis Brinley.
		John Cushing.			Capt. Jeremiah Fisher.
		John Wheelwright.			Daniel Tast.
		Benjamin Lynde.	1729.	Aug. 28.	Jacob Wendell.
		Addington Davenport.			Maj. Leonard Vassall.
		Thomas Hutchinson.			Richard Bill.
		Samuel Brown.		Dec. 12.	Jonathan Wade.
		Thomas Fitch.		Dec. 20.	John Quincy.
		Edmund Quincy.	1729-30.	Mch. 19.	Nathaniel Saltonstall.
		Adam Winthrop.	1731.	Dec. 29.	Hon. William Tailer.
		Jonathan Dowse.			Nathaniel Byfield.
		Joseph Hammond.			Edward Bromfield.
		Paul Dudley.			Addington Davenport.
		Samuel Thaxter.			Thomas Hutchinson.
		John Turner.			Thomas Fitch.
		Spencer Phips.			Edmund Quincy.
		Daniel Oliver.			Adam Winthrop.
		Symonds Epes.			Elisha Cooke.
		Meletiah Bourne.			Paul Dudley.
		John Stoddard.			Samuel Thaxter.
		John Chandler.			Daniel Oliver.
		Timothy Lindall.			Thomas Palmer.
		Charles Chambers.			Edward Hutchinson.
		Theophilus Burrill.			William Dudley.

[1] Of Wrentham.   [2] Over the Indians in the county.

Justices of the Peace—Continued.

1731.	Dec. 29.	William Clarke.	1734.	June 28.	Joshua Winslow.
		John Alford.			Isaac Royal.
		Joseph Wadsworth.		July 3.	Thomas Tilestone.
		Thomas Cushing.		Dec. 31.	Benjamin Lincoln.
		John Osborn.	1734–5.	Feb. 21.	John Fisher, Jr.
		Ezekiel Lewis.	1735.	June 27.	John Hunt.
		Josiah Willard.	1735–6.	Jan. 9.	Nathaniel Green.*
		Samuel Checkley.			John Bowles.*
		John Nelson.			Jonathan Ware.*
		Anthony Stoddard.			Samuel White.*
		Samuel Sewall.			Samuel Sewall*
		John Quincy.			Hugh Hall.*
		Timothy Clark.		16.	Francis Borland.
		Elijah Danforth.	1736.	June 22.	Edward Clark.
		John Jekyll.		Dec. 22.	Oliver Hayward.
		Thomas Steel.	1737.	Oct. 25.	Jeremiah Fisher.
		John Ruck.			Benjamin Bird.
		Joshua Lamb.	1737–8.	Mch. 9.	John Doane.
		Robert Spurr.			Andrew Belcher.
		John Ballentine.	1738.	Aug. 12.	Paul Dudley.
		Stephen Minot.	1738–9.	Jan. 12.	Byfield Lyde.*
		Nathaniel Green.		25.	Caleb Lyman.
		John Bowles.			Joshua Cheever.
		Jonathan Ware.			Andrew Oliver.
		Francis Brinley.		26.	Samuel Miller.
		Jacob Wendell.			Daniel Henchman.
		Leonard Vassall.			Thomas Hubbard.
		Richard Bill.	1740.	June 28.	Oxenbridge Thatcher.
		Nathaniel Saltonstall.			Nathaniel Balstone.
		John Colman.			Thomas Hutchinson.
		Andrew Faneuil.			John Erving.
		James Bowdoin.		Nov. 5.	Abiel Walley.*
		William Foye.			William Tyley.*
		Samuel Welles.		Dec. 5.	Jonas Clark.
		James Pemberton.	1741.	July 16.	Zabdiel Boylston.
		Samuel Sewall.			Joseph Gooch.
		Job Lewis.			Samuel Swift.
		Henry Deering.		21.	Joseph Crosby.
		Samuel White.		Dec. 31.	Eliakim Hutchinson.
1732.	July 6.	Habijah Savage.	1743.	June 27.	Francis Brinley.*
		George Bethune.		Oct. 20.	Edward Winslow.*
	7.	John Walley.	1743–4.	Mch. 1.	William Downe.
	Dec. 15.	Joseph Heath.			Cornelius Waldo.
		Samuel Adams.			George Rodgers.
		John Metcalf.		5.	John Jeffries.*
	28.	William Tyler.			William Foye.*
1733.	Oct. 26.	Benjamin Dyer.			Samuel Waldo.*
1734.	June 28.	John Fayerweather.			Thomas Cushing.
		William Stoddard.		6.	James Minot.*
		Samuel Watts.			William Lawrence.*

Justices of the Peace—Continued.

1744.	Aug. 18.	John Yeamans.*
	Nov. 1.	Joseph Heath.*
1745-6.	Feb. 8.	Samuel White.*
		Samuel Adams.
		William Stoddard.
		Henry Sewall.
	12.	Jeremiah Gridley.*
		John Metcalf.
1746.	Aug. 5.	Adam Cushing.
1746-7.	Jan. 14.	Henry Adams.
1747.	June 27.	Edward White.
	Dec. 12.	Samuel Cushing.
1747-8.	Meh. 1.	Isaac Gridley.
1748.	Apr. 14.	John Hill.
	May 17.	Jeremiah Green.
	Nov. 8.	Henry Atkins.
	15.	John Clark.
	18.	Nathaniel Oliver, Jr.
		Robert Spurr.
1748-9.	Jan. 4.	John Shephard.
		Eliphalet Pond.
	—— 11.	Timothy Prout.
1749.	Aug. 12.	Ezekiel Goldthwait.
	Aug. 18.	Charles Paxton.
	Sept. 8.	John Fayerweather.*
		Joshua Winslow.*
		Jacob Royall.*
1749-50.	Jan. 18.	Thomas Palmer.
1750.	Apr. 26.	Joseph Heath.*
1751.	June 21.	Ebenezer Fisher.
		Jeremiah Adams.
1752.	Feb. 7.	Thomas Hubbard.*
		John Wendell.
		Edmund Quincy.
		Foster Hutchinson.
		Joshua Henshaw.
		Ebenezer Pierpoint.
	Apr. 7.	William Stoddard.*
1753.	Jan. 2.	Joseph Richards.*
	Jan. 3.	Samuel Miller.*
	Sept. 6.	Thomas Oxnard.
1754.	Jan. 25.	Caleb Loring.
		William Skinner.
	Apr. 19.	James Boutineau.
		Benjamin Lincoln.*
	Apr. 20.	Thomas Greene.
		Zechariah Johonnot.
1755.	Jan. 8.	Joseph Green.
		James Bowdoin.
	June 26.	George Cradock.*

1755.	June 26.	Joseph Green.
		Ebenezer Storer.
		Thomas Goldthwait.
		Joseph Williams.
	Oct. 10.	Stephen Greenleaf.
		Andrew Oliver.
		Harrison Gray.
1756.	July 9.	Joseph Lee.
		Isaac Winslow.
	July 27.	Richard Clarke.
		James Pitts.
	Sept. 14.	Daniel Henchman.*
		John Phillips.*
		Henry Lloyd.
		Thomas Flucker.
		John Erving.
		Robert Temple.
		Peter Chardon.
		Thomas Gunter.
		John Jones.
		Samuel Wentworth.
		Richard Dana.
		Joseph Jackson.
		James Otis.
		Nathaniel Hatch.
		Jacob Cushing.
		Meletiah Bourn.
		George Talbot.
1757.	Jan. 3.	Richard Dana.*
		Samuel Grant.
		Jonathan Simpson.
		Shrimpton Hutchinson.
		Samuel Niles.
	Aug. 26.	Josiah Quincy.
1758.	Jan. 11.	Ebenezer Miller.
		Nathaniel Sumner.
	May 12.	Belcher Noyes.
		Royall Tyler.
		Samuel Welles, Jr.
1759.	Meh. 8.	Nicholas Boylston.
		Eleazer Williams.
		John Gould.
	Dec. 19.	John Rowe.
		John Ruddock.
		Arnold Welles.
		Joseph Coffin.
		John Brown.
1760.	May 23.	Sylvester Gardiner.
		Joseph Sherburne.
		Thomas Tyler.

Justices of the Peace—Continued.

1760.	May 23.	William Blair Townsend.	1761.	Nov. 5.	Joshua Henshaw.
		Thomas Cushing.			James Boutineau.
		John Scollay.			Thomas Green.
		Samuel Hewes.			Zechariah Johonnot.
		Benjamin Austin.			Joseph Green.
		James Foster.			Thomas Goldthwait.
	Nov. 13.	Nathaniel Bethune.			Joseph Williams.
		Cotton Tufts.			Andrew Oliver, Jr.
		Thomas Savage.			Joseph Lee.
1761.	Nov. 5.	John Osborne.*			Isaac Winslow.
		Eliakim Hutchinson.*			Richard Clarke.
		Benjamin Lincoln.*			James Pitts.
		Francis Brinley.*			Henry Lloyd.
		Joshua Winslow.*			John Erving, Jr.
		Jacob Royall.*			Robert Temple.
		George Cradock.*			Peter Chardon.
		Andrew Belcher.*			John Jones.
		Byfield Lyde.*			Samuel Wentworth.
		Jeremy Gridley.*			Samuel Grant.
		John Phillips.*			Jonathan Simpson.
		Sylvester Gardiner.*			Shrimpton Hutchinson.
		Richard Dana.*			Samuel Niles, Jr.
		Foster Hutchinson.*			Joseph Jackson.
		Stephen Greenleaf.*			James Otis, Jr.
		Ezekiel Goldthwait.*			Jacob Cushing.
		Samuel Winthrop.*			Meletiah Bourne.
		Benjamin Dyer.			Josiah Quincy.
		Francis Borland.			Ebenezer Miller, Jr.
		Jeremiah Fisher.			Nathaniel Sumner.
		Oxenbridge Thatcher.			Belcher Noyes.
		Nathaniel Balston.			Royall Tyler.
		Zabdiel Boylston.			Samuel Welles, Jr.
		Joseph Gooch.			Nicholas Boylston.
		Henry Sewall.			Eleazer Williams.
		Henry Adams.			John Gould (of Hull.)
		John Steele.			John Rowe.
		Edward White.			Arnold Welles.
		Isaac Gridley.			Thomas Cushing.
		John Hill.			John Scollay.
		Jeremiah Green.			Samuel Hewes.
		Henry Atkins.			Benjamin Austin.
		John Clark.			Joseph Sherburne.
		Robert Spurr.			Thomas Tyler.
		Joseph Dowse.			William Blair Townsend.
		Eliphalet Pond.			James Foster.
		Charles Paxton.			Nathaniel Bethune.
		Ebenezer Fisher.			Cotton Tufts.
		Jeremiah Adams.			Joseph Hewins.
		John Wendell.			William Phillips.
		Edmund Quincy.			James Humphries.

Justices of the Peace—Continued.

1761.	Nov. 5.	Benjamin Fenno.	1764.	May 2.	Joshua Henshaw.*
		Benjamin Pemberton.		June 8.	Samuel Pemberton.
		Isaac Gardner, Jr.		Oct. 10.	Benjamin Hallowell, Jr.
		John Borland.	1765.	Feb. 6.	John Thaxter.
		Edward Hutchinson.		June 6.	John Hancock.
		Joshua Clap.		June 26.	Ebenezer Thayer, Jr.
		Joseph Gardner.		Sept. 11.	William Tucker.
		Thomas Fayerweather.		Oct. 30.	John Metcalf.
		William Story.	1766.	Jan. 1.	Stephen Miller.
		William Bowdoin.	1767.	Jan. 7.	William Hyslop.
		Josiah Newhall.		Mch. 25.	Jonathan Williams.
		Thomas Deering.			Thomas Hutchinson, Jr.
	Nov. 12.	John Osborn.*			John Jones.
		John Erving.*		Aug. 5.	Francis Bernard.
		James Bowdoin.*			Nathaniel Rogers.
		Thomas Hancock.*		Oct. 7.	Joseph Harrison.
		Thomas Flucker.*		Dec. 2.	George Erving.
		William Stoddard.*	1768.	Jan. 13.	Bela Lincoln.
		John Ruddock.*		Feb. 24.	Elijah Dunbar.
		Nathaniel Hatch.*		Oct. 26.	James Murray.
		Jonathan Whitney.		Dec. 7.	James Murray,*
		Elisha Tilestone.			William Coffin, Jr.
		John Barret.	1769.	Feb. 1.	Robert Auchmuty.*
		John Gooch.			Joshua Loring.
		Samuel Dexter.		Apr. 5.	Joshua Loring.*
		John Waldo.			John Bernard.
		Joseph Dudley.	1770.	May 9.	John Winslow.
1762.	Jan. 28.	Josiah Quincy.*			Thomas Gray.
		Samuel Cushing.	1771.	Jan. 10.	Edmund Quincy.*
		Joseph Crosby.		Mch. 21.	Samuel Quincy.
		John Leverett.		Dec. 10.	Elisha Hutchinson.
		Ezekiel Lewis.	1772.	Apr. 23.	Elisha Niles.
		John Avery.		June 4.	John Gray.
		Samuel Fitch.		June 17.	Thomas Alleyne.
	Feb. 4.	Eliphalet Pond.*		Aug. 12.	Nathaniel Perkins.
		Benjamin Greenleaf.			James Lloyd.
		George Abbot, Jr.			Thomas Bulfinch.
		Ebenezer Barker.		Oct. 1.	John Hill.*
	Mch. 11.	Isaac Smith.			Joseph Williams.*
		Samuel Sewall.			Miles Whitworth.
		Benjamin Lincoln.		Dec. 31.	Patrick Tracey.
		Elisha Adams.			Stephen Hooper.
	May 14.	John Spooner.	1773.	Sept. 29.	Henry Adams.*
1763.	Feb. 17.	William Holden.			Belcher Noyes.*
		William Spurr.	1774.	Mch. 4.	George Bethune.
		Thomas Dudley.			Benjamin Gridley.
	Feb. 24.	Nathaniel Wheelwright.			Nathaniel Taylor.
		William White.			Edward Lyde.
		John Tudor.			Samuel Barrett.
	July 6.	Roger Hale.			

Justices of the Peace—Continued.

ESSEX.

1692.	May 27.	Maj. William Browne.*	1715.	Dec. 9.	Stephen Sewall.
		Benjamin Browne.			Nehemiah Jewett.
		John Woodbridge.			Joseph Woodbridge.
		Capt. John Appleton.*			John Dummer.
		Capt. Daniel Epps.			John Newman.
		Capt. Daniel Pierce.			Robert Hale.
		Capt. John Higginson.			John Turner.
		Capt Dudley Bradstreet.*			John Brown.
		Capt. Thomas Wade.			John White.
		Simon Wainwright.		Dec. 24.	Edward Brattle.
1696.	Oct. 16.	John Appleton, Jr.			James Cawley.
1699.	July 17.	Col. John Wainwright.	1717.	Nov. 12.	Symonds Epes.
1700.	June 7.	Maj. Thomas Noyes.			Daniel Rogers.
		Capt. John Legg.	1717–18.	Feb. 13.	John Wainwright.
		Capt. Nathaniel Norden.	1718.	June 27.	Joseph Woodbridge.
1701.	June 12.	Capt. John Burrill.		Nov. 20.	John Cawley.
1702.	June 30.	Col. Nath'l Saltonstall.	1719.	Nov. 25.	William Bradbury.
		Lt. Col. Dud. Bradstreet.			Richard Kent.
		Maj. Robert Pike.		Dec. 9.	Capt. Benjamin Stevens.
		Col. John Wainwright.			Capt. Azor Gale.
		Maj. Thomas Noyes.	1720.	July 15.	Timothy Lindall.
		Capt. John Legg.		Dec. 19.	Epes Sargeant.
		Capt. Nathaniel Norden.	1720–1.	Mch. 31.	Thomas Hale.
		Samuel Appleton.	1721–2.	Mch. 9.	Theophilus Burrill.
		Capt. John Burrill.	1722.	June 29.	Richard Currier.
		William Hirst.		July 3.	William Gedney.
		Robert Hale.	1722–3.	Jan. 9.	Thomas Berry.
		Joseph Woodbridge.	1724.	June 23.	Joseph Woodbridge.*
		Capt. Samuel Browne.	1724–5.	Feb. 18.	Edward Sargeant.
		Josiah Wolcott.	1725.	Sept. 2.	Richard Saltonstall.
1703.	June 5.	Maj. Francis Wainwright.	1726.	June 7.	Walter Price.
1704.	June 15.	Maj. Stephen Sewall.			John Oulton.
		John Wainwright.*			Daniel Epes.
		Thomas Noyes.*	1726–7.	Feb. 23.	Maj. Mathew Whipple.
1706.	Nov. 8.	John Newman.	1727.	June 17.	John Wainwright.*
1707.	June 5.	Maj. Richard Saltonstall.		Dec. 26.	Orlando Bagley, Jr.
	Dec. 4.	Nehemiah Jewett.	1727–8.	Jan. 24.	John Dummer.*
1708–9.	Feb. 25.	Daniel Epes.		Feb. 22.	Stephen Minot.
1711.	June 15.	John Dummer.			Joshua Orne.
1715.	Dec. 9.	William Browne.	1728.	June 18.	Maj. Joseph Gerrish.
		John Hathorne.			Capt. Henry Rolfe.
		Jonathan Corwin.	1729.	Apr. 10.	Benjamin Lynde, Jr.
		Samuel Appleton.		Oct. 10.	John Appleton.
		Daniel Epps.			Thomas Noyes.
		William Hirst.			John Dummer.
		John Legg.			John Wainwright.
		John Burrill.			William Bradbury.
		Josiah Wolcott.			Benjamin Stevens.

Justices of the Peace—Continued.

1729.	Oct. 10.	Richard Kent.	1733.	June 22.	——— White.
		Epes Sargeant.			Robert Hale.
		Thomas Hale.			Thomas Lambert.
		William Gedney.			Abraham Howard.
		Thomas Berry.			Joseph Blaney.
		Edward Sargeant.		July 17.	James Lindall.
		Richard Saltonstall.			William Fairfax.
		Walter Price.			Samuel Barnard.
		John Oulton.			John Higginson.
		Daniel Epes.			John Walcott.
		Orlando Bagley.		Oct. 26.	John March.
		Stephen Minot, Jr.			Jonathan Wade.
		Joshua Orne.			Jonathan Cogswell.
		Joseph Gerrish.			John Baker.
		Henry Rolfe.	1733-4.	Feb. 14.	John Choat.
		Benjamin Lynde, Jr.		Feb. 28.	Samuel Lee.
		Daniel Appleton.	1731.	Apr. 23.	John Osgood.
		Joseph Atkins.		June 28.	Ammi Ruhamah Wise.
	Dec. 5.	Mathew Whipple.			Benjamin Rolfe.
		James Cawley.		Dec. 27.	Benjamin Browne.
		Nathaniel Saltonstall.			Daniel Epes.*
1733.	June 22.	John Appleton.			Benjamin Lynde, Jr.*
		Benjamin Lynde.		Dec. 31.	Thomas Kimball.
		John Turner.	1735.	June 27.	Richard Rogers.
		Symonds Epes.	1735-6.	Jan. 2.	Charles Pierce.*
		Theophilus Burrill.			Andrew Burleigh.
		James Cawley.			Joseph Allen.
		John Dummer.	1736.	June 22.	David Wood.
		John Wainwright.		——— 23.	Daniel Appleton.*
		William Bradbury.	1737.	June 30.	Joseph Blaney.*
		Richard Kent.			Edward Kitchen.
		Epes Sargeant.		Oct. 25.	John Hobson.
		Thomas Berry.		Nov. 10.	Benjamin Marston.*
		Edward Sargeant.		Dec. 29.	Epes Sargeant.*
		Mathew Whipple.			Benjamin Browne.*
		Richard Saltonstall.			John Greenleaf.
		John Oulton.	1738.	July 8.	Samuel Moody, Jr.
		Daniel Epes.			James Skinner.
		Orlando Bagley.	1738-9.	Jan. 26.	John Turner.
		Joshua Orne.	1739.	Oct. 5.	Benjamin Gerrish.
		Joseph Gerrish.			John Frost.
		Henry Rolfe.	1740.	Apr. 4.	Orlando Bagley.*
		Benjamin Lynde, Jr.		July 5.	Samuel Barton.
		Daniel Appleton.	1741.	Apr. 2.	Thomas Hale.
		Joseph Atkins.		July 21.	Thomas Rowell.
		Thomas Barton.	1743-4.	Mch. 1.	William Browne.*
		Joshua Bayley.			John Greenleaf.*
		Ichabod Plaisted.	1744.	Aug. 18.	Daniel Mansfield.
		Charles Peirce.			William Atkins.
		Mitchel Sewall.	1744-5.	Jan. 12.	Joseph Swett.

Justices of the Peace—Continued.

1744–5.	—— 19.	John Choate.*		1758.	Jan. 11.	Jonathan Bagley.
	Jan. 19.	Robert Hale.			May 12.	Thomas Woodbridge.
1745.	Apr. 26.	Caleb Cushing.				Richard Saltonstall
1745–6.	Jan. 24.	Benjamin Pickman.		1759.	Mch. 8.	Ichabod Plaisted.*
	Feb. 8.	John Turner.				Humphrey Hobson.
1746.	Aug. 5.	William Collins.				Joseph Gerrish, Jr.
1747.	Aug. 19.	John Tasker.				Benjamin Newhall.
	Sept. 11.	Andrew Burleigh.		1761.	Nov. 19.	John Choate.*
1748.	Sept. 27.	Epes Sargeant, Jr.				Caleb Cushing.*
		Robert Hooper, Jr.				Nathaniel Ropes.*
	Nov. 8.	Samuel Rogers.				Andrew Oliver, Jr.*
		Benjamin Marston.*				Epes Sargent.*
	Nov. 18.	Jacob Fowle.				Daniel Epes.*
1749.	Apr. 21.	Daniel Epes, Jr.				Ichabod Plaisted.*
	June 29.	David Moseley.				Thomas Rowell.*
		Joseph Bowditch.				Benjamin Pickman.*
	Sept. 8.	John Peaslee.				Jacob Fowle.*
		Thomas Norton.				Samuel Phillips.*
1752.	Feb. 7.	Daniel Gibbs.				William Bourn.*
	Apr. 3.	Daniel Farnham.				Robert Hooper, Jr.*
	Sept. 19.	Samuel Phillips, Jr.				Robert Hale.*
1753.	Jan. 2.	Henry Gibbs.				William Browne.*
		Samuel White.				John Browne.*
	Jan. 3.	Timothy Pool.				Charles Pierce.*
	Aug. 24.	Robert Hooper, Jr.*				Joseph Gerrish.
	Sept. 6.	John Tasker.*				Joseph Atkins.
	Sept. 14.	Joshua Orne, Jr.				Joseph Blaney.
1754.	Jan. 25.	Daniel Gibbs.				Samuel Barnard.
	Apr. 19.	William Browne.				John Hobson.
	—— 20.	John Greenleaf.*				Nathan Hale.
1755.	Jan. 8.	Benjamin Jones.				John Osgood.
		William Stevens.				William Atkins.
		James Davis.				Daniel Witham.
		Thomas Saunders.				William Collins.
		Francis Choat.				Samuel Rogers.
	Oct. 10.	John Leach.				Daniel Epes, Jr.
1756.	July 27.	Richard Lechmere.				Joseph Bowditch.
		John Higginson.				Nathaniel Peaslee.
	Sept 14.	Samuel Curwin.				Daniel Farnum.
		John Nutting.				Samuel White.
		John Lee.				Benjamin Jones.
		Nathaniel Allen.				Francis Choate.
		William Bourn.				James Davis.
		Richard Greenleaf.				John Leach.
		Michael Dalton.				Samuel Curwin.
		Isaac Morrill.				John Lee.
		James McHard.				Isaac Merrill.
1758.	Jan. 11.	Samuel Gardner.				James McHard.
		Jeremiah Lee.				William Stevens.
		Stephen Higginson.				Nathaniel Allen.

Justices of the Peace—Continued.

1761.	Nov. 19.	Benjamin Prescott.	1762.	Apr. 21.	Nathan Bowen.
		Michael Dalton.			William Vans.
		Humphrey Hobson.	1763.	Feb. 17.	Nathaniel Brown.
		Benjamin Newhall.			Samuel Plummer.
		John Higginson.			Dudley Atkins.
		John Nutting.		July 6.	Jacob Fowle, Jr.
		Richard Greenleaf.			James Cockle.
		Samuel Gardner.		Dec. 7.	William Browne.
		Jeremiah Lee.	1764.	May 2.	John Osgood, Jr.
		Jonathan Bagley.		Oct. 25.	Daniel Farnum.
		Thomas Woodbridge.		Nov. 7.	Thomas Geary.
		Richard Saltonstall.	1765.	Apr. 3.	Joseph Frye.
		Joseph Coffin.		June 20.	Stephen Emery.
		John Brown.		Oct. 30.	Peter Frye.
		Thomas Saunders, Jr.		Nov. 6.	Ebenezer Putnam.
		Epes Sargent, Jr.			Joseph Blaney.
		Daniel Gibbs.	1766.	July 9.	Samuel Greenleaf.
		Joshua Orne.		Oct. 1.	John Gallison.
		Joseph Gerrish, Jr.	1767.	Mch. 25.	Nath'l Peaslee Sargent.
		John Turner.		July 1.	Azor Orne.
		Samuel Barton.		Sept. 2.	Benjamin Pickman, Jr.
		Aaron Potter.	1768.	Jan. 6.	Joseph Dowse.
		Joseph Appleton.			William Story.
		Thomas Gage.			Samuel Moody.
		Benjamin Mulliken.		Aug. 3.	Francis Cabot.
		Nathaniel Henchman, Jr.	1769.	May 3.	Samuel Cotnam.
		William Brown, Jr.		July 12.	John Lowell.
		Edw'd A'gustus Holyoke.		July 26.	John Cushing.
		John Chipman.	1770.	May 9.	Thomas Roby.
	Nov. 20.	Benjamin Marston.	1771.	Apr. 12.	Ebenezer Burrill.
		William Pynchon.			Richard Derby, Jr.
		Isaac Mansfield.		Apr. 19.	John Calef.
		James Athearn.	1772.	Jan. 15.	William Browne.*
		Jonathan Allen.			Peter Frye.
	Dec. 4.	Josiah Fairfield.			Benjamin Harris.
1762.	Jan. 28.	Aaron Wood.			Nathaniel Carter.
	Feb. 4.	Joseph Blaney.*			Tristram Dalton.
		Samuel Rogers.			Micajah Sawyer.
	Mch. 1.	Joseph Bowditch.*		Mch. 18.	Dummer Jewett.
		Jerahmeel Bowers.*		Oct. 1.	Stephen Barker.
		Thomas Gilbert.		Nov. 25.	Abner Cheever.
	Apr. 21.	William Epes.			

MIDDLESEX.

1692.	May 27.	Thomas Danforth.*	1692.	May 27.	Jonathan Tyng.
		William Bond.*			Capt. Thomas Browne.
		William Johnson.*			Capt. James Minot.
		Maj. Thomas Henchman.		Dec. 7.	Ephraim Flint.

Justices of the Peace—Continued.

1699.	July 17.	John Leverett.
1700.	June 7.	Maj. James Converse.
1702.	June 30.	Jonathan Tyng.
		John Leverett.
		Samuel Hayman.
		Capt. Francis Foxcroft.
		Maj. James Converse.
		Ephraim Flint.
		Capt. Thomas Browne.
		Capt. James Minot.[1]
		Capt. Joseph Morse.
	Oct. 23.	Capt. James Minot.
		Capt. John Browne.
		Jonas Bond.
		Edward Emerson.
1707.	Apr. 15.	Capt. Thomas Howe.
1710.	June 8.	Thomas Oliver.
	June 22.	John Usher.
1713.	June 5.	Capt. Nathaniel Carey.
		Lt. Col. Spencer Phips.
	Aug. 27.	Capt. Jonas Prescott.
1714.	June 15.	Maj Joseph Buckminster.
		Capt. Hopestill Brown.
1715.	Apr. 7.	Capt. Jonathan Pool.
	Dec. 9.	John Usher.
		Jonas Bond.
		Thomas How.
		Nathaniel Cary.
		Spencer Phips.
		Joseph Buckminster.
		Hopestill Brown.
		Jonas Prescott.
		Charles Chambers.
		Henry Phillips.
	Dec. 13.	Samuel Gooking.
		Jonathan Dowse.
	Dec. 24.	James Minot.
		Jonathan Poole.
1716.	June 15.	Oliver Whiting.
1718.	Apr. 16.	Francis Fulham.[3]
	June 27.	Capt. John Foye.
		Thomas Tufts.
1719.	June 27.	John Menzies.
		Thomas Greaves.
1720.	Dec. 19.	John Leverett.[3]
		Henry Flint.[3]
1720-1.	Mch. 31.	Francis Bowman.
1721.	Nov. 15.	Eleazer Tyng.

1721.	Nov. 15.	Eleazer Flagg.
	Nov. 16.	William Briant.
1722.	June 29.	John Jekyll.
1723.	Sept. 6.	Francis Foxcroft, Jr.
1724.	Dec. 15.	Jonathan Prescott.
		Ebenezer Stone.
1724-5.	Feb. 19.	Saville Sympson.
1725.	Sept. 2.	John Alford.
		Daniel Russell.
1726-7.	Feb. 23.	Benjamin Poole.
1727.	Dec. 26.	Joseph Wilder.
		Jonathan Poole.
		Benjamin Prescott.
1727-8.	Jan. 24.	William Ward.
1729.	Aug. 22.	Nathaniel Danforth.
		Maj. William Brattle.
	Aug. 28.	John Whitman.
	Oct. 10.	Jonathan Remington.
		Nathaniel Cary.
		James Minot.
		Hopestill Brown.
		Henry Phillips.
		Francis Fulham.
		Joseph Buckminster.
		John Houghton.
		Thomas Greaves.
		Francis Bowman.
		Eleazer Tyng.
		William Bryant.
		John Jekyll.
		Francis Foxcroft.
		Jonathan Prescott.
		Benjamin Poole.
		Daniel Russell.
		Jonathan Poole.
		Joseph Wilder.
		Benjamin Prescott.
		William Ward.
		Jonas Clark.
		Benjamin Wood.
	Dec. 5.	Oliver Whiting.
		Samuel Danforth.
		William Brattle.
		John Whitman.
		Capt. John Flynt.
		John Richardson.
	Dec. 12.	Samuel Gookin.
1729-30.	Mch. 19.	Capt. Nathaniel Sartle.

[1] Rejected.   [2] Over the Indians.
[3] Both for the town of Cambridge, for the regulation and government of Harvard College.

Justices of the Peace—Continued.

1731.	July 9.	Spencer Phips.	1736.	June 22.	Benjamin Thompson.
		Jonathan Remington.		Dec. 22.	Joseph Blanchard.
		Jonathan Dowse.			Francis Wells.
		Charles Chambers.	1737.	July 2.	Joseph Bowman.
		James Minot.		Nov. 10.	Henry Flynt.
		Hopestill Brown.		—— 18.	Isaac Royall.*
		Francis Fulham.		Dec. 29.	Nathaniel Saltonstall.*
		Oliver Whiting.	1738-9.	Jan. 12.	Edmund Trowbridge.*
		Joseph Buckminster.			Jonas Prescott.
		Thomas Greaves.		—— 26.	Samuel Jackson.
		Francis Bowman.	1739.	Dec. 21.	William Lawrence.
		Eleazer Tyng.	1740.	June 28.	Chambers Russell.
		John Jekyll.	1740-1.	Jan. 9.	Sampson Stoddard.
		Francis Foxcroft.	1743-4.	Mch. 1.	Ezekiel Cheever.*
		Daniel Russell.			John Jones.*
		Jonathan Pool.			Isaac Royall.
		Benjamin Pool.			James Gooch.
		Benjamin Prescott.		—— 8.	Simon Tufts.*
		Benjamin Wood.	1744.	Apr. 5.	Joseph Lemmon.*
		Samuel Danforth.			Rowland Cotton.*
		William Brattle.		Aug. 18.	Thomas Read.
		John Whitman.			Joseph Lynde.
		John Flynt.		Nov. 1.	Joseph Bucknam.
		John Richardson.	1745.	Dec. 20.	Richard Dana.*
		Nathaniel Sartle.	1746.	Aug. 5.	William Read.
		Thomas Jenner.		—— 9.	Henry Gibbs.
		John Greenwood.			Josiah Bremer.
	July 16.	Richard Foster.			Thomas Lambert.
1732.	July 6.	Joseph Lemon.	1747.	June 27.	Jonathan Prescott.
	July 7.	Andrew Boardman.			Thomas Greenwood.
	Dec. 15.	Kendal Parker.		Aug. 19.	John Winthrop.
1733.	May 4.	Capt. Ephraim Curtis.	1748.	Apr. 6.	Thomas Jenner.*
	Oct. 26.	John Jones.		Nov. 18.	Cadwallador Ford.
1733-4.	Feb. 14.	Stephen Hall.	1748-9.	Jan. 11.	Jonas Bond.
		Ebenezer Roby.	1749.	Apr. 18.	Barnard Townsend.
		Joseph Mason.			Joseph Buckminster.
		Nathaniel Harris.		Aug. 18.	Thaddeus Mason.
	Feb. 28.	Simon Tufts.		Sept. 8.	Thomas Kidder.
1734.	Apr. 23.	John Death.	1749-50.	Jan. 18.	Henry Vassall.
	Dec. 27.	John Mason.	1751.	June 21.	Samuel Brooks.
		John Vinton.	1752.	Feb. 7.	David Phips.
1734-5.	Feb. 21.	Ephraim Williams.	1753.	Jan. 2.	Henry Gibbs.*
1735.	June 27.	Ezekiel Cheever.			Robert Temple.
1735-6.	Jan. 2.	Benjamin Prescott.*			Joseph Haven.
	Jan. 16.	Samuel Danforth.*			Simpson Jones.
		William Brattle.*			James Prescott.
1736.	June 22.	Daniel Russell.*		Jan. 3.	Josiah Converse.
		Samuel Dummer.			Samuel Livermore.
		James Minot.			Ebenezer Nichols.
		Samuel Cary.			Oliver Fletcher.

Justices of the Peace—Continued.

1753.	Aug. 24.	Francis Foxcroft.*
		Francis Fulham.*
		Isaac Royal.*
	Sept. 13.	Joseph Mason.
		Simpson Jones.
1754.	Jan. 25.	Eleazer Tyng.*
		Benjamin Read.
		Josiah Converse.
	Apr. 19.	Joseph Bowman.
		Isaac Coolidge.
		Nathaniel Russell.
1755.	Jan. 8.	Thomas Whiting.
	June 26.	Josiah Johnson.
		John Hunt.
		Stephen Hall.
1756.	July 27.	Ezekiel Cheever.
	Sept. 14.	James Russell.
		Elisha Jones.
1757.	Aug. 26.	Ralph Inman.
1758.	May 12.	Thomas Sparhawk.
	Aug. 1.	Samuel Livermore.*
1759.	Mch. 8.	Charles Prescott.
1760.	May 23.	Caleb Dana.
	Nov. 13.	Joseph Lee.
1761.	Nov. 20.	Francis Foxcroft.*
		Andrew Boardman.*
		William Lawrence.*
		Eleazer Tyng.*
		Daniel Russell.*
		John Jones.*
		Samuel Livermore.*
		Ezekiel Cheever.*
		Oliver Fletcher.*
		Charles Prescott.*
		John Tyng.*
		James Russell.*
		Isaac Royall.*
		John Whitman.
		Ebenezer Roby.
		Joseph Bowman.
		Samuel Brigham.
		Thomas Reed.
		William Reed.
		Josiah Brown.
		Jonathan Prescott.
		Thomas Greenwood.
		Thaddeus Mason.
		Thomas Kidder.
		Samuel Brooks.
		Cadwallader Ford.

1761.	Nov. 20.	Joseph Haven.
		Ebenezer Nichols.
		Henry Vassall.
		Simpson Jones.
		James Prescott.
		Benjamin Reed.
		Isaac Bowman.
		Thomas Whiting.
		Joseph Buckminster.
		John Hunt.
		Josiah Johnson.
		Elisha Jones.
		Stephen Hall.
		Joseph Lee.
		Caleb Dana.
		Ezekiel Cheever, Jr.
		Ralph Inman.
		Thomas Sparhawk.
		John Winthrop.
		David Phips.
		Sampson Stoddard.
		Bela Lincoln.
		John Noyes.
		Benjamin Faneuil.
		Robert Temple.
		Richard Lechmere.
		Henry Gardner.
		James Fowle.
	Dec. 4.	Ezra Green.
		Jonathan Hastings.
1762.	Jan. 28.	Jonathan Sewall.
		Samuel Cary.
	Mch. 25.	Isaac Rand.
1763.	Feb. 21.	Elisha Jones.*
	July 6.	William Stickney.
	Sept. 9.	Josiah Converse.
1764.	Apr. 4.	William Kneeland.
	May 2.	Joseph Lee.*
	June 8.	Samuel Henley.
		Abel Lawrence.
	Nov. 7.	Thaddeus Mason.*
1765.	Feb. 6.	Ephraim Spaulding.
	June 6.	John Beton.
		John Cummings.
	Oct. 30.	John Borland.
1766.	June 18.	Jere. Dummer Rogers.
	July 2.	Joseph Perry.
		Henry Barnes.
	Oct. 1.	Richard Cary.
1767.	Mch. 25.	Charles Russell.

Justices of the Peace—Continued.

1767.	Mch. 25.	John Varnum.	1771.	Dec. 10.	John Denny.
	Sept. 2.	Edward Sheaffe.			David Cheever.
1768.	Feb. 21.	John Wilson.			John Foxcroft.
1769.	Mch. 1.	William Baldwin.			Leonard Williams.
	May 3.	John Apthorp.			Sampson Stoddard.
		Thomas Oliver.			Andrew Newell.
1770.	May 9.	John Vassall.	1773.	Aug. 11.	Daniel Bliss.
	Aug. 30.	Simon Tufts.			Thomas Russell.
	Sept. 17.	William Pepperrell.			James Tyng.
		Charles Pelham.			Thomas Brattle.
		Abraham Fuller.			Thomas Danforth.
1771.	Apr. 12.	John Read.			John White.
	—— 16.	Jonas Prescott.			Duncan Ingraham.
	—— 19.	Jonas Dix.	1774.	Feb. 3.	Samuel Bancroft.

HAMPSHIRE.

1692.	May 27.	Maj. John Pynchon.*	1729.	Oct. 10.	Henry Dwight.
		Peter Tilton.*			Samuel Barnard.
		Capt. Aaron Cooke.			Ebenezer Porter.
		Joseph Hawley.			Thomas Hastings.
		Capt. Samuel Partridge.*		Dec. 5.	Capt. Thomas Kellogg.
	Dec. 8.	John Holyoke.		Dec. 20.	William Pynchon.
1696.	Oct. 16.	Joseph Parsons.	1732.	Dec. 28.	Samuel Partridge.
1699.	July 17.	Joseph Parsons.			John Stoddard.
1702.	June 29.	Joseph Hawley.			John Pynchon.
		Joseph Parsons.			John Ashley.
		Capt. Aaron Cooke.			Eleazer Porter.
		John Holyoke.			William Pynchon.
		John Pynchon, 2d.			Joseph Kellogg.
1707.	Dec. 5.	Samuel Porter.			Timothy Dwight.
1710–11.	Mch. 23.	Maj. John Stoddard.			John Kent.
1713.	Oct. 27.	Capt. Jonathan Wells.			Joseph Lord.
1715.	Dec. 10.	Aaron Cooke.	1731.	Dec. 31.	Thomas Wells.
		John Stoddard.	1734–5.	Feb. 21.	William Pynchon, Jr.
		Jonathan Wells.	1735.	June 27.	Ebenezer Pomroy.*
		John Pynchon, Jr.			John Sherman.
1716.	June 15.	John Ashley.	1736.	Dec. 29.	Israel Williams.
1719.	June 27.	Henry Dwight.	1738–9.	Jan. 12.	Joseph Pynchon.*
1722–3.	Jan. 9.	Samuel Barnard.	1739.	Oct. 5.	Richard Cronch.
1723.	Sept. 6.	Joseph Jennings.	1710.	July 12.	William Pynchon.*
1725.	Sept. 2.	Ebenezer Porter.	1743.	June 23.	John Stoddard.*
1727.	Dec. 26.	Dr. Thomas Hastings.			Ebenezer Pomroy.*
1729.	Oct. 10.	Samuel Partridge.			John Ashley.*
		John Stoddard.			Eleazer Porter.*
		John Pynchon.			Timothy Dwight.*
		Joseph Parsons.			Joseph Kellogg.
		John Ashley.			Thomas Wells.
		Jonathan Wells.			William Pynchon.

Justices of the Peace—Continued.

1743.	June 23.	John Sherman.
		Thomas Ingersoll.
		Israel Williams.
		Joseph Pynchon.
		Ephraim Williams.*
		Richard Crouch.
1743–4.	Mch. 1.	Elijah Williams.
	Mch. 6.	Joseph Pynchon.*
	Mch. 13.	Thomas Ingersoll.*
1747–8.	Feb. 16.	Seth Field.
	Mch. 10.	Samuel Dwight.
		Josiah Dwight.
1748.	Apr. 23.	John Worthington.
	Nov. 15.	Phinehas Lyman.
	Nov. 18.	William Williams.
1749.	June 29.	Joseph Hawley.
	Sept. 8.	David Ingersoll.
1751.	June 21.	John Worthington.*
1753.	Jan. 2.	Elijah Williams.*
		John Ashley.
	—— 3.	Noah Ashley.
	—— 4.	Joseph Dwight.*
	Sept. 13.	Timothy Dwight.*
		Elijah Williams.*
		Seth Field.
1754.	Jan. 25.	Josiah Dwight.*
	Apr. 19.	Samuel Mather.
		Thomas Williams.
1755.	June 26.	Israel Ashley.
		Jabez Ward.
	Oct. 10.	Eldad Thayer.
1756.	July 9.	Josiah Chauncy.
		Timothy Woodbridge.
	Sept. 14.	John Mascarene.
1758.	June 22.	Timothy Dwight, Jr.
		Eleazer Porter.
1759.	Mch. 8.	Eldad Taylor.

1759.	Mch. 8.	Charles Phelps.
		Edward Pynchon.
	Dec. 19.	Edward Pynchon.*
1760.	May 23.	Gideon Lyman.
1762.	Feb. 4.	John Sherman.
		Seth Field.
		David Moseley.
		Samuel Mather.
		Thomas Williams.
		Josiah Chauncey.
		Eleazer Porter.
		Eldad Taylor.
		Timothy Dwight.*
		John Worthington.*
		Elijah Williams.*
		Josiah Dwight.*
		Joseph Hawley.*
		Timothy Dwight, Jr.*
	Mch. 25.	Edward Pynchon.
		Gideon Lyman.
		Daniel Burt.
1765.	June 20.	William Williams.
1768.	Feb. 24.	Simon Strong.
1769.	Feb. 1.	Oliver Partridge.*
	May 3.	Moses Bliss.
1770.	May 9.	Jonathan Ashley.
		Jonathan Bliss.
		James Bridgham.
		John Wood.
		Timothy Robinson.
1771.	Apr. 12.	Moses Bliss.*
		Elisha Porter.
		John Ingersoll.
1772.	June 19.	Joseph Root.
		William Billing.
		Abraham Burbank.

PLYMOUTH.

1692.	May 27.	Capt. Nath'l Thomas.*
		Ephraim Morton.*
		John Cushing.*
		John Wadsworth.
		Capt. Thomas Howard.
1696.	Oct. 16.	Isaac Little.
1699.	July 17.	Isaac Little.
		William Brett.
1700.	June 7.	John Cushing, Jr.

1700.	June 7.	Capt. James Warren.
		Isaac Winslow.
		Elihu Brett.
1702.	June 30.	John Cushing, Sr.
		Elihu Brett.
1708–9.	Feb. 25.	Capt. Seth Arnold.
		James Warren.[1]
		Joseph Morse.[1]
1711.	Apr. 19.	John Cushing.*

[1] Over the Indians, and to join with them two of the principal Indians of the several tribes.

Justices of the Peace—Continued.

1711.	Apr. 19.	James Warren.*
1712.	June 5.	Capt. Josiah Edson.
1715.	Dec. 9.	Nathaniel Thomas, Jr.
		Josiah Edson.
		John Bradford.
	Dec. 13.	Samuel Prince.
	—— 21.	Benjamin Warren.[1]
1716.	June 15.	Isaac Little.[1]
		Shearjashub Bourne.[2]
1717.	Nov. 12.	Isaac Little.[1]
		Benjamin Warren.[1]
1717–18.	Feb. 13.	Joshua Cushing.
1718.	Nov. 20.	Thomas Turner.
1719.	June 27.	John Barker.
	Dec. 9.	John Watson.
1720.	July 22.	Jacob Thompson.
1721–2.	Mch. 9.	Isaac Lothrop.
1726.	June 7.	Edward Winslow.
		Edward Arnold.
1727.	June 27.	Josiah Cotton.*
1729.	July 10.	John Cushing, Jr.
	Oct. 10.	John Cushing.
		Nathaniel Thomas.
		Josiah Edson.
		Josiah Cotton.
		Isaac Little.
		Joshua Cushing.
		John Barker.
		John Watson.
		Isaac Lothrop.
		Edward Winslow.
		Edward Arnold.
		John Cushing, Jr.
		Nicholas Sever.
		Isaac Little.[1]
		Benjamin Warren.[1]
		Josiah Morton.[1]
	Dec. 5.	John Little.
1731.	July 23.	Ezra Clapp.[1]
	Aug. 25.	Isaac Winslow.
		John Cushing.
		Nathaniel Thomas.
		Josiah Edson.
		Josiah Cotton.
		Isaac Little.
		Joshua Cushing.
		John Watson.
		Isaac Lothrop.

1731.	Aug. 25.	Edward Arnold.
		John Cushing, Jr.
		Nicholas Sever.
		John Little.
		Amos Turner.
		Isaac Little.[1]
		Benjamin Warren.[1]
		Josiah Morton.[1]
	Dec. 23.	Edward Winslow.
1731–2.	Mch. 21.	Nathaniel Thomas, Jr.
		James Warren.
1733.	June 22.	Kenelm Winslow.
1733–4.	Feb. 14.	Samuel Pool.
	Feb. 24.	David Little.
	Feb. 28.	Caleb Loring.
1734.	June 28.	John Thomas.
	July 3.	Elisha Bysby.
	Dec. 27.	Thomas Bryant.
		Elijah Cushing.
		Samuel Bartlett, Jr.
1735–6.	Jan. 9.	Thomas Croad.
1736.	June 22.	Elkanah Leonard.
1737.	June 30.	Joseph Thomas.
	Oct. 25.	John Alden.
1737–8.	Jan. 13.	John Cushing.*
1738–9.	Jan. 25.	John Winslow.
1740.	July 5.	Daniel Johnson.
	Nov. 5.	David Little.*
1744.	Aug. 18.	Peter Oliver.
	Nov. 1.	Robert Brown.
1744–5.	Jan. 19.	George Leonard.*
1745–6.	Jan. 24.	Edward Winslow.
1746.	Aug. 9.	Isaac Lothrop.
1747.	June 27.	Josiah Edson, Jr.
		Thomas Foster.
1747–8.	Mch. 1.	Israel Fearing.
1748.	May 17.	Peter Oliver.*
		Isaac Lothrop.
1748–9.	Jan. 4.	Nathaniel Clapp.
	Jan. 11.	Daniel Howard.
1749.	Aug. 18.	David Stockbridge.
	Sept. 8.	John Watson.
1751.	Apr. 24.	Thomas Foster.*
		Edward Winslow.*
	June 21.	Elijah Cushing.*
1753.	Sept. 6.	Josiah Cotton.*
	—— 13.	Thomas Croade.
1754.	Jan. 25.	Samuel Pool.

[1] Over the Indians.
[2] Over the Indians at Sandwich.

Justices of the Peace—Continued.

1751.	Jan. 25.	George Watson.
	Apr. 19.	David Stockbridge.*
		John Cushing.*
		David Little.*
1755.	Jan. 11.	Ezra Clapp.[1]
	June 26.	John Fearing.
		Barnabas Shurtliff.
1756.	Sept. 14.	Kenelm Winslow.
		Abijah White.
		James Warren.*
1758.	Jan. 11.	Noah Sprague.
1760.	May 23.	James Hovey.
		Israel Turner.
	Oct. 31.	Gideon Bradford.
		Joseph Tinkham.
		Josiah Keen.
		John Cushing, Jr.
1762.	Jan. 28.	Gamaliel Bradford.*
		Nicholas Sever.*.
		John Winslow.*
		Elijah Cushing.*
		Thomas Foster.*
		Edward Winslow.*
		Thomas Croade.*
		David Little.*
		Joseph Cushing.*
		David Stockbridge.*
		Daniel Johnson.*
		Josiah Edson.*
		John Cushing, Jr.*
		John Little.
		Samuel Bartlett.
		Robert Brown.
		Daniel Howard.
		George Watson.
		Nathaniel Clapp.
		John Willis.

1762.	Jan. 28.	Abijah White.
		Kenelm Winslow.
		Noah Sprague.
		John Fearing.
		James Hovey.
		Josiah Keen.
		Gideon Bradford.
		Joseph Tinkham.
		Nathaniel Ray Thomas.
		John Cotton.
		William Sever.
		Ephraim Keith.
		William Watson.
		Thomas Mayhew.
		Nathaniel Ruggles.
		Samuel Norton.
1763.	Feb. 17.	Briggs Alden.
		Daniel Oliver.
1764.	Feb. 1.	Josiah Sturtevant, Jr.
	June 8.	James Hovey.*
1765.	Feb. 6.	Joseph Greenleaf.
1766.	Feb. 5.	Joseph Jocelyn.
1767.	Aug. 5.	Nathan Howard.
1768.	Mch. 16.	Peter Oliver, Jr.
1769.	Jan. 4.	Nathan Cushing.
1770.	Aug. 30.	John Thomas.
1771.	June 27.	Josiah Cushing.
		Pelham Winslow.
1772.	Jan. 15.	Daniel Howard.*
		George Watson.*
		Nathaniel Clapp.*
	June 4.	Josiah Torrey.
	Oct. 21.	Samuel Sprague.
1773.	Mch. 2.	Charles Stockbridge.
	Sept. 29.	Edward Winslow, Jr.
1774.	Feb. 10.	Enoch Hammond.

BRISTOL.

1692.	May 27.	John Saffin *
		Capt. John Brown.*
		Capt. Thomas Leonard.*
		Nicholas Peck.
		Joseph Church.
		Capt. Seth Pope.
1699.	July 17.	Nathaniel Payne.
1700.	June 7.	Ebenezer Brenton.

1702.	June 29.	Maj. Benjamin Church.
		Nicholas Peck.
		Nathaniel Payne.
		Joseph Church.
		Thomas Tabor.
	Oct. 23.	Henry Mackintosh.
1707.	Nov. 8.	Capt. Seth Pope.
1708-9.	Feb. 25.	Joseph Church.

[1] Over the Indians.

Justices of the Peace—Continued.

1708-9.	Feb. 25.	Seth Pope.	1729.	Oct. 10.	Nathaniel Payne.
1710.	Aug. 24.	Samuel Newman.			Sylvester Richmond.
		Thomas Church.			Timothy Fales.
1712.	June 4.	Capt. Samuel Walker.			Samuel Vyal.
		Capt. Jared Talbot.			Samuel Brown.
1713.	June 5.	Capt. George Leonard.			Samuel Willis.
		Benjamin Church.[1]			William Southward.[1]
1713-14.	Feb. 22.	Seth Williams.		Dec. 5.	Nathaniel Hubbard.
1714.	June 15.	James Church.[2]	1733.	June 22.	Job Almy.[1]
		Benjamin Numpas.[2]			Thomas Church.[1]
		Zaccheus Gouge.[2]			Sylvester Richmond.[1]
		John Nantos.[2]			Seth Williams.
		Obadiah Bryant.[2]			Jared Talbot.
		Nathan Tobe.[2]			Thomas Church.
		Isaac Simons.[2]			Nathaniel Blagrove.
		Samuel Homes.[2]			Job Almy.
1715.	Dec. 10.	Benjamin Church.			Nathaniel Hubbard.
		Seth Pope.			Thomas Terry.
		Henry Hodges.			George Leonard.
		Jared Talbot.			Sylvester Richmond.
		Daniel Smith.			Timothy Fales.
		John Rogers.			Samuel Willis.
		Job Almy.			Jonathan Woodbury.
1717.	Nov. 12.	William Southward.[1]			Thomas Bowen.
		Job Almy.[1]			Samuel Allen.
		Seth Pope.[1]			Joseph Mason.
1722-3.	Jan. 9.	Sylvester Richmond.[1]			Samuel Leonard.
1723-4.	Mch. 4.	George Leonard.		Oct. 26.	Lemuel Pope.[1]
	—— 19.	Nathaniel Payne.	1733-4.	Feb. 28.	Stephen Payne.
1724.	June 23.	Timothy Fales.	1734.	Dec. 27.	Samuel Williams.
	Dec. 2.	Sylvester Richmond.			Perez Bradford.
		Samuel Vyall.			Sylvester Richmond, Jr.
	—— 15.	Samuel Brown.	1735-6.	Jan. 2.	Ephraim Leonard.
1726.	June 7.	Samuel Willis.			John Foster.
1728.	June 18.	Nathaniel Hubbard.*	1736.	Dec. 22.	Nathaniel Blagrove.*
		Nathaniel Payne.*	1737.	June 30.	Edward Howard.
	June 21.	Richard Harden.		Dec. 29.	Philip Tabor.
1729.	Aug. 22.	Thomas Church.[1]	1738.	Aug. 12.	Gershom Crane.
		Job Almy.[1]	1738-9.	Jan. 12.	Timothy Fales.*
		Sylvester Richmond.[1]		Jan. 26.	William Hall.
	Oct. 10.	Simon Davis.	1739.	Oct. 5.	Samuel Howland.
		Jared Talbot.	1740.	July 5.	Joseph Allen.
		Seth Williams.	1743-4.	Mch. 1.	Seth Williams.*
		Thomas Church.			Nathaniel Hubbard.*
		Nathaniel Blagrove.			Thomas Church.*
		Job Almy.			Nathaniel Blagrove.*
		Henry Hodges.			Job Almy.*
		Thomas Terry.			Thomas Torrey.*
		George Leonard			Sylvester Richmond.*

[1] Over the Indians.   [2] All Indians, over the Indians.

Justices of the Peace—Continued.

1743-4.	Mch. 1.	Timothy Fales.*	1760.	May 23.	George Godfrey.
		Stephen Payne.*			Jerathmeel Bowers.
		Perez Bradford.*	1761.	Nov. 24.	George Leonard.*
		Sylvester Richmond, Jr.*			Ephraim Leonard.*
		Samuel Willis.*			James Williams.*
		Thomas Bowen.			Zephaniah Leonard.*
		Ephraim Leonard.			Samuel Willis.*
		John Foster.			Thomas Bowen.*
		Edward Howard.			Timothy Fales.*
		Philip Tabor.			Samuel White.*
		William Hall.			Gershom Crane.
		Samuel Howland.			Ebenezer Hathaway.
		Samuel Leonard, Jr.			Daniel Carpenter.
		Joseph Russell.			Ezra Richmond.
		William Richmond.			George Leonard, Jr.
		John Godfrey.			Elisha Tobey.
		Samuel White.			Aaron Kingsley.
		Stephen West.			Jerathmeel Bowers.
1746-7.	Jan. 14.	William Canady.			George Godfrey.
1747.	June 27.	Gershom Crane.			Abiel Torrey.
		Ephraim Leonard.*			Thomas Morey.
	Dec. 12.	Eseck Brown.			Benjamin Akin.
1747-8.	Mch. 1.	Josiah Talbot.			Stephen Fuller.
1748.	Apr. 15.	Samuel Willis.*			Daniel Williams.
		Thomas Bowen.*	1762.	Jan. 28.	Benjamin Williams.
	Nov. 8.	Zephaniah Leonard.		Apr. 21.	George Leonard, Jr.*
		Ebenezer Hathaway.			Thomas Cobb.
	Dec. 28.	James Williams.*	1763.	Feb. 24.	William Bullock.
1749.	Apr. 18.	Moses Howe.		Sept. 7.	Robert Treat Paine.
	Aug. 12.	Daniel Carpenter.	1765.	Feb. 6.	George Brightman.
	—— 18.	Ezra Richmond.	1766.	June 18.	Elisha Tobey.*
1754.	Jan. 25.	George Leonard, Jr.		Nov. 12.	Ebenezer Crane.
	Apr. 19.	Abiel Torrey.	1767.	July 1.	Daniel Leonard.
1755.	Jan. 8.	Zephaniah Leonard.		Nov. 4.	Robert Luscom.
		John Foster.	1768.	Feb. 24.	Zephaniah Leonard.
1756.	Sept. 14.	Samuel White.*	1772.	June 17.	Walter Spooner.*
		Thomas Gilbert.			Edward Pope.
		Aaron Kingsley.		July 14.	George Godfrey.*
		Elisha Tobey.	1774.	Feb. 3.	George Wheaton.
		William Slade.			

BARNSTABLE.

1692.	May 27.	Maj. John Freeman.*	1702.	June 29.	John Otis.
		Capt. John Thatcher.*			Jonathan Sparrow.
		Capt. John Gorham.*			Maj. John Gorham.
		Stephen Skiffe.	1707.	June 5.	Nathaniel Freeman.
		Capt. Jonathan Sparrow.		—— 10.	Joseph Doane.
		Shearjashub Bourn.	1708-9.	Feb. 25.	John Otis.
1702.	June 29.	Stephen Skiffe.			Joseph Doane.

Justices of the Peace—Continued.

1710.	Aug. 24.	Capt. Thomas Paine.	1729.	Oct. 10.	Thomas Payne.
1713.	June 5.	John Doane.			Shubael Baxter.
		Daniel Parker.			Joseph Crocker.[1]
	Aug. 12.	Samuel Sturges.			*John Thomas.*
		Peter Thatcher.			*Joshua Ralph.*[1]
1715.	Dec. 10.	John Gorham.		Dec. 20.	Maj. John Thatcher.
		Joseph Doane.	1731.	Aug. 25.	Meletiah Bourne.
		William Bassett.			Peter Thatcher.
		Peter Thatcher.			Nathaniel Freeman.
		Samuel Sturges.			Samuel Sturges.
		John Doane.			Joseph Doane.
	Dec. 21.	John Gorham.[1]			John Doane.
		William Bassett.[1]			Joseph Lothrop.
		Joseph Doane.[1]			Hezekiah Doane.
		Peter Thatcher.[1]			Ezra Bourne.
1716.	June 15.	John Otis.[1]			Edmund Freeman.
		Shearjashub Bourne.[1]			Thomas Payne.
1717.	Nov. 12.	John Otis.[1]			Shubael Baxter.
		William Bassett.[1]			John Thatcher.
		Peter Thatcher.[1]			Thomas Clark.
		Joseph Doane.[1]			Meletiah Bourne.[1]
1717–18.	Feb. 13.	John Bacon.			Peter Thatcher.[1]
1719.	June 27.	John Thomas.[1]			Joseph Doane.[1]
		Joshua Ralph.[1]			Nathaniel Freeman.[1]
1721–2.	Mch. 9.	Joseph Lothrop.			Shubael Baxter.[1]
	·	Joseph Crocker.[1]			Joshua Crocker.[1]
1722.	June 29.	Meletiah Bourne.[1]			*John Thomas.*[1]
1723.	Sept. 6.	Hezekiah Doane.			*Joshua Ralph.*[1]
		Ezra Bourne.[1]		Dec. 23.	John Russell.
1724.	Dec. 15.	Nathaniel Freeman.[1]	1733.	May 4.	John Davis.
1725.	Dec. 18.	Ezra Bourne.		June 22.	Ebenezer Lewis.
1727.	Dec. 26.	Edmund Freeman.			David Crocker.
1727–8.	Feb. 22.	Thomas Payne.	1733–4.	Feb. 14.	John Sturges.
1729.	Apr. 10.	Shubael Baxter.			James Otis.
	Aug. 22.	Meletiah Bourne.[1]			Sylvanus Bourne.
		Peter Thatcher.[1]	1734.	Dec. 27.	Joseph Doane.*
		Joseph Doane.[1]			Stephen Skiffe.[1]
		Ezra Bourne.	1735.	June 27.	Joseph Robinson.
		Nathaniel Freeman.	1736.	June 22.	Samuel Sturges, Jr.
		Shubael Baxter.	1737.	June 30.	William Payne.
	Oct. 10.	Nathaniel Freeman.		July 2.	Stephen Skiffe.
		Samuel Sturges.	1738–9.	Jan. 12.	John Otis.*
		Joseph Doane.		—— 25.	John Thatcher.*
		John Doane.		—— 26.	Seth Parker.
		John Bacon.	1739.	Dec. 21.	John Russell.*
		Joseph Lothrop.	1740.	Apr. 4.	Joseph Freeman.
		Hezekiah Doane.	1740–1.	Jan. 21.	Judah Thatcher.
		Ezra Bourne.	1741.	July 16.	John Hallet.
		Edmund Freeman.	1742.	July 8.	Joseph Lothrop.[1]

[1] Over the Indians.

Justices of the Peace—Continued.

1743.	June 27.	Shubael Gorham.*		1762.	Jan. 21.	Roland Cotton.*
1743–4.	Mch. 1.	Samuel Jennings.				David Gorham.*
1744.	Dec. 21.	Silas Bourne.				Thomas Smith.*
1744–5.	Jan. 3.	Samuel Tupper.[1]				Edward Bacon.*
1746–7.	Jan. 14.	Solomon Lombard.				John Gorham.*
		Solomon Otis.				Judah Thatcher.*
1747.	June 27.	Nathaniel Stone, Jr.				Silas Bourne.*
		Rowland Robinson.				Solomon Otis.*
	Sept. 11.	Thomas Winslow.				Roland Robinson.*
1747–8.	Feb. 16.	David Graham.				John Freeman.*
	Mch. 1.	David Crocker.*				Kenelm Winslow.*
		Sylvanus Bourne.*				Nathaniel Stone.
		James Otis.*				Samuel Smith.
		Samuel Knowles.				Samuel Tupper.
		Samuel Smith.				Barnabas Paine.
1748.	Nov. 8.	John Hallet.				Isaac Hinckley.
		Samuel Tupper.				Nymphas Marston.
1753.	Jan. 2.	Barnabas Payne.				Jonathan Doane.
	Jan. 3.	David Gorham.*		1764.	Feb. 1.	Joseph Otis, Jr.*
		John Freeman.*				Chillingworth Foster, Jr.
	Sept. 11.	Benjamin Crocker.[1]		1765.	June 26.	Thomas Freeman.[1]
	—— 13.	Thomas Winslow.*		1767.	Mch. 25.	Isaac Hinckley.
		John Sturges.*				David Thatcher.
1754.	Apr. 19.	Kenelm Winslow.		1768.	Feb. 24.	Daniel Hall.
1755.	June 26.	Rowland Cotton.*			Aug. 3.	Meletiah Bourne.
	Sept. 14.	Isaac Hinckley.		1770.	May 9.	Daniel Davis.
1758.	Aug. 3.	Thomas Smith, Jr.*		1771.	July 18.	Elisha Doane.
		Edward Bacon.				Thomas Bourne.
1760.	May 23.	Nymphas Marston.				John Greenough.
1762.	Jan. 21.	Ezra Bourne.*		1772.	July 29.	Nymphas Marston.*
		John Thatcher.*		1773.	Mch. 2.	Shearjashub Bourne.
		Sylvanus Bourne.*			Sept. 29.	Richard Bourne.
		Thomas Winslow.*				

YORK.

1692.	May 27.	Francis Hooke.*		1711.	June 8.	Capt. John Hill.
		Maj. Charles Frost.*		1713.	Aug. 27.	Capt. Samuel Moody.
		Samuel Wheelwright.*			Oct. 27.	Charles Frost.
		Abraham Preble.		1715.	Dec. 15.	Elisha Plaisted.
		Roger Kelley.		1716.	June 15.	John Watts.[2]
		William Lakeman.		1717.	Nov. 12.	John Watts.
1694–5.	Mch. 6.	William Pepperrell.		1717–18.	Feb. 13.	Ephraim Savage.
1700.	June 7.	John Wheelwright.		1718.	June 27.	Capt. John Penhallow.
1701.	June 12.	Capt. Ichabod Plaisted.		1719.	Nov. 25.	Capt. John Gray.
1702.	June 30.	Samuel Donnell.		1721–2.	Mch. 9.	Joseph Hill.
		William Pepperrell.		1724.	June 23.	William Pepperrell.
1703.	Aug. 5.	David Phippen.				Samuel Came.
1706.	Dec. 13.	John Plaisted.		1726.	June 2.	Nathaniel Gerrish.

[1] Over the Indians. [2] At Arrowsic.

Justices of the Peace—Continued.

1726.	June 2.	Joseph Heath.	1743.	Sept. 9.	Jabez Bradbury.
1728.	June 18.	Capt. Samuel Jordan.	1744.	Aug. 18.	Jeremiah Powell.
1729.	Apr. 11.	Timothy Gerrish.	1744-5.	Feb. 9.	Nathaniel Sparhawk.
	June 25.	Capt. Joshua Moody.			Joseph Noyes.
	Oct. 10.	William Pepperrell.		Mch. 21.	Nathaniel Sparhawk.*
		John Gray.	1745.	Dec. 20.	Simon Frost.
		Joseph Hill.	1747.	June 27.	Daniel Moulton, Jr.
		Samuel Came.		Sept. 11.	Nathaniel Donnell.
		Joseph Heath.	1747-8.	Mch. 10.	John Oulton.
		Joshua Moody.			Samuel Moody.
		Timothy Gerrish.	1748.	Apr. 11.	John Fox.
		Samuel Jordan.		—— 23.	Elihu Gunnison.*
		John Gyles.			John Storer.*
	Dec. 5.	Joseph Moody.			Charles Frost.*
1729-30.	Mch. 18.	Humphrey Chadbourn.			Samuel Small.
1731.	July 16.	John Wheelwright.			Samuel Sewall.
		William Pepperrell, Jr.		Nov. 15.	Thomas Perkins.
		Timothy Gerrish.	1749.	Apr. 21.	Timothy Prout.
		Thomas Westbrook.			Rishworth Jordan.
		John Gray.			John Willis.
		Samuel Came.	1751.	June 21.	Simon Frost.*
		John Gyles.			Moses Pierson.
		Joseph Moody.	1752.	Apr. 3.	Jonas Mason.
		Joseph Sawyer.	1753.	Jan. 3.	Edward Milliken.
		John Hill.			Benjamin Parker.
		Elihu Gunnison.		Sept. 6.	Samuel Denny.*
		Roger Deering.		Sept. 13.	Jeremiah Powell.
	—— 23.	Joseph Heath.			Jonas Mason.
	Sept. 9.	John Minot.			Moses Pierson.
		Samuel Seaberry.			Christopher Strout.
	Dec. 23.	Joshua Moody.	1751.	Jan. 25.	William Lithgow.
		Samuel Denny.			John North.
1732.	Dec. 15.	Henry Wheeler.			Jonathan Bane.
1733.	May 4.	Capt. Thomas Smith.			John Minot.
	July 17.	David Cargil.			Jabez Bradbury.
		John North.			Edward Milliken.
1733-4.	Feb. 21.	Nicholas Shapleigh.			Samuel Moody.
	—— 28.	Joseph Hill.		Apr. 19.	Timothy Prout.
1734.	July 3.	Benjamin Larrabee.	1755.	Jan. 8.	Aaron Hinckley.
		James Woodside.			Joseph Storer.
	Dec. 31.	Richard Cutt, Jr.		June 26.	Samuel Hill.
1735.	June 27.	John Powell.	1756.	Sept. 14.	Joseph Sayer.*
1736.	Dec. 29.	Peter Nowell.			Ezekiel Cushing.*
1737.	Nov. 10.	John Noyes.			John Bradbury.
		Thomas White.	1757.	Jan. 3.	Joseph Sawyer.*
1738-9.	Jan. 12.	Charles Frost.	1758.	Jan. 11.	Samuel Waldo.
	—— 26.	John Storer.			Thomas Bragdon.
1739.	July 6.	Samuel Denny.*	1759.	Mch. 9.	Foxwell Curtis Cutt.
1740.	Nov. 5.	Christopher Strout.		Dec. 19.	Nathaniel Donnell.
1741.	Apr. 2.	Alexander Bulman.	1760.	May 23.	Benjamin Chadbourne.

Justices of the Peace—Continued.

1760.	May 23.	Nathaniel Wells.
		Charles Hill.
1761.	Nov. 20.	Joseph Sayer.*
		Richard Cutt.*
		John Storer.*
		Daniel Moulton.*
		Jeremy Moulton.*
		Simon Frost.*
		John Hill.*
		John Frost.*
		Rishworth Jordan.*
		Samuel Sewall.
		Joseph Storer.
		Nathaniel Donnell.
		Thomas Bragdon.
		Benjamin Chadbourne.
		Nathaniel Wells.
		Charles Hill.
		John Bradbury.
		Edward Cutt.
		Jonathan Sayward.
		Charles Chauncey.
		Thomas Perkins.
		Samuel Moody.
1761.	Nov. 20.	James Gowen.
		Jeremiah Hill.
		Samuel Jordan.
1765.	Feb. 6.	Benjamin Parker.
		Jonathan Bane.
		John Wheelwright.
	Sept. 11.	Jeremiah Moulton.*
1767.	Jan. 7.	Thomas Cutts.
	Nov. 4.	David Sewall.
1768.	Jan. 6.	Jonathan Sayward.*
	June 2.	James Gowen.*
	June 30.	Samuel Sewall, Jr.
1769.	July 26.	Joseph Storer.*
1770.	May 23.	Joseph Simpson, Jr.
	June 21.	Joseph Frye.
	Aug. 30.	Tristram Jordan.
		Job Lyman.
1771.	Apr. 12.	Jotham Moulton.*
1771.	Feb. 3.	Nathan Lord.
	Mch. 4.	James Gowen.*
		Jonathan Sayward.*
		Nathaniel Welles, Jr.
		James Sullivan.

NANTUCKET.

1692.	May 27.	Capt. John Gardner.*
		James Coffin.
		William Geere.
		William Worth.
1707.	Nov. 8.	Capt. Richard Gardner.
		James Coffin.[1]
1711.	June 8.	George Gardner.
1712.	Oct. 24.	George Bunker.
1715.	Sept. 10.	George Bunker.[1]
		Ebenezer Coffin.[1]
	Dec. 13.	Same two.
1719.	June 27.	Same two.
1728.	June 18.	Joseph Gardner.
1729.	Oct. 10.	Ebenezer Coffin.[1]
		George Bunker.[1]
		George Gardner.
		George Bunker.
		John Coffin.
		Joseph Gardner.
		Ebenezer Coffin.
1732.	July 6.	George Bunker.
		George Gardner.
		John Coffin.
		Joseph Gardner.
1732.	July 6.	George Bunker.[1]
1744.	Dec. 21.	Josiah Coffin.*
1744-5.	Jan. 3.	Thomas Brock.*
1747.	Sept. 11.	Jeremiah Gardner.
		George Gardner.
		Josiah Coffin.
		Thomas Brock.
		Jonathan Coffin.
		Grafton Gardner.
		John Bunker.
		Ebenezer Calef.
1751.	June 21.	John Bunker.*
1754.	Jan. 25.	Abishai Folger.
1761.	Nov. 12.	Obed Hussey.
	—— 20.	Jeremiah Gardner.*
		Josiah Coffin.*
		Jonathan Coffin.*
		Grafton Gardner.*
		Caleb Bunker.*
		Ebenezer Calef.
		Abishai Folger.
		Obed Hussey.
1771.	Dec. 10.	Timothy Folger.

[1] Over the Indians.

Justices of the Peace—Continued.

DUKES.

1692.	May 27.	Mathew Mayhew.*	1733.	May 4.	Zaccheus Mayhew.
		Thomas Mayhew.			Enoch Coffin.
		Simeon Athearn.			John Allen.
	July 18.	John Coffin.			Samuel Norton.
	Dec. 8.	Richard Sarson.			Benjamin Smith.
1696.	Oct. 16.	John Coffin.			Simeon Butler.
1698.	June 3.	Capt. Benjamin Skiffe.	1731.	Dec. 31.	Ebenezer Norton.
1701.	June 12.	Benjamin Smith.	1744.	Dec. 21.	John Sumner.
	.	Joseph Norton.	1747-8.	Mch. 1.	John Athearn.
1707.	June 5.	Thomas Mayhew.[1]	1748.	Apr. 15.	Paine Mayhew.
1708-9.	Feb. 25.	Thomas Mayhew.			Zaccheus Mayhew.*
1713.	June 5.	John Worth.[3]			Enoch Coffin.*
	Oct. 27.	Enoch Coffin.			John Allen.*
		Paine Mayhew.			John Sumner.*
1715.	Sept. 16.	Ebenezer Allen.*			Samuel Norton.
	Dec. 10.	Enoch Coffin.			John Norton.
		Zaccheus Mayhew.			Ebenezer Norton.
		Benjamin Smith.[2]			Jabez Athearn.
1719.	June 27.	Thomas Lathrop.	1754.	Jan. 25.	John Coffin.[1]
1720.	July 22.	John Worth.		Apr. 19.	Ebenezer Smith.
1722.	July 3.	Benjamin Hawse.	1761.	Oct. 16.	John Allen.*
		John Chipman.			John Sumner.*
1723.	Sept. 6.	John Chipman.			Ebenezer Smith.*
1724.	Dec. 15.	Zaccheus Mayhew.			John Newman.*
1729.	Oct. 10.	Paine Mayhew.			Josiah Tilton.*
		Ebenezer Allen.			Mathew Mayhew.*
		Enoch Coffin.			Jabez Athearn.
		Benjamin Smith.			Nathaniel Hancock.
		Zaccheus Mayhew.	1762.	Mch. 11.	Zaccheus Mayhew.
		John Worth.	1764.	June 8.	John Worth.
		Thomas Lothrop.[1]	1771.	June 12.	Enoch Coffin.
		John Chapman.[1]		Dec. 10.	Joseph Mayhew.*
		Zaccheus Mayhew.[1]			James Athearn.*
1733.	May 4.	Zaccheus Mayhew.[1]			Shubael Cottle.
		John Allen.[1]			

WORCESTER.

1731.	June 30.	John Chandler.	1731.	June 30.	Josiah Willard.
		Joseph Wilder.			Daniel Taft.
		William Ward.			Samuel Dudley.
		William Jennison.			Nahum Ward.
		John Chandler, Jr.			Henry Lee.
		Benjamin Willard.	1732.	July 7.	William Clark.
		Samuel Wright.			Samuel Willard.
		Joseph Dwight.	1733.	May 1.	Capt. John Keyes.

[1] Over the Indians.   [2] And also for the Indians.   [3] "So that he lay down his Tavern.

Justices of the Peace—Continued.

1733.	Oct. 26.	Edward Hartwell.
1735-6.	Jan. 16.	John Chandler, Jr.*
1737.	June 30.	Richard More.
	Oct. 25.	James Wilder.
1738-9.	Jan. 25.	John Martin.
1743-4.	Mch. 1.	Joseph Wilder.*
		Joseph Dwight.*
		John Chandler.*
		William Ward.*
		Samuel Willard.*
		Nahum Ward.*
		Daniel Taft.
		Edward Hartwell.
		John Keyes.
		Richard Moor.
		Jonas Rice.
		Josiah Converse.
		Thomas Gilbert.
		Samuel Chandler.
		Thomas Steel.
		John Harwood.
		Samuel Willard, Jr.
1744.	Dec. 21.	Edward Hartwell.*
		Thomas Prentice.
	— 27.	Oliver Wilder.
		Edward Baker.
1745-6.	Jan. 21.	Peter Atherton.
1746.	Aug. 5.	Samuel Lyscomb.
1747.	June 27.	Joseph Wilder, Jr.
		John Chandler, Jr.
1748.	Nov. 15.	Noah Ashley.
		Isaac Barnard.
		Robert Goddard.
1749.	Aug. 12.	John Hazelton.
		Charles Brigham.
1751.	June 21.	Artemas Ward.
		William Rawson.
1753.	Jan. 2.	William Richardson.
	Sept. 13.	Daniel Taft.
1754.	Jan. 25.	John Stone.
		John Murray.
		Duncan Campbell.
		William Ayres.
		Jedediah Foster.
		Moses Marey.
		William Down.
	Apr. 19.	Timothy Ruggles.
		John Whitcomb.
		Joseph Lord.
1755.	Jan. 8.	Timothy Payne.

1755.	Jan. 8.	Nathan Tyler.
1758.	Jan. 11.	Timothy Payne.*
		Josiah Brewer.
		James Putnam.
1760.	May 23.	Timothy Brigham.
		Simeon Dwight.
		David Osgood.
1762.	Jan. 21.	John Chandler.*
		William Ward.*
		Edward Hartwell.*
		Timothy Ruggles.*
		Timothy Payne.*
		Thomas Steel.*
		Joseph Wilder.*
		Artemas Ward.*
		John Murray.*
		Jedediah Foster.*
		James Putnam.*
		John Keyes.
		Josiah Converse.
		John Harwood.
		Edward Baker.
		Oliver Wilder.
		Peter Atherton.
		Isaac Barnard.
		Robert Goddard.
		John Hazelton.
		Charles Brigham.
		William Richardson.
		Duncan Campbell.
		Moses Marey.
		William Ayres.
		John Stone.
		Nathan Tyler.
		John Whitcomb.
		John Caldwell.
		Josiah Brewer.
		David Osgood.
		Simeon Dwight.
		John Eliot.
		Ezra Taylor.
		Edward Davis.
		Abijah Willard.
		Joshua Willard.
		Daniel Henshaw.
		Benjamin Goodridge.
		Thomas Wilder.
	Aug. 26.	John Chandler.*
1763.	Feb. 17.	Francis Whipple.
	Mch. 3.	Solomon Wood.

Justices of the Peace—Continued.

1766.	Feb. 5.	Josiah Wolcott.
	Dec. 10.	Jedediah Marcy.
1767.	Mch. 25.	Henry Bromfield.
		Daniel Bliss.
1768.	Jan. 13.	Daniel Oliver.
	Feb. 24.	John Chandler, Jr.
		Joseph Dorr, Jr.
		Israel Taylor.
		William Barron.
1769.	Jan. 4.	Gardner Chandler.
	May 3.	Abel Willard.*
1769.	May 3.	Thomas Legget.
	July 12.	Joshua Upham.
1771.	Nov. 4.	Charles Cushing.*
1772.	Mch. 18.	Jonathan White.
		Levi Willard.
		Ephraim Woolson.
		Samuel Wilder.
		John Muzzy.
		Thomas Brigdon.
1774.	Feb. 3.	Ezra Houghton.

LINCOLN.

1760.	Oct. 31.	Samuel Dennie.*
		William Lithgow.*
		Aaron Hinckley.*
		John North.*
		William Cushing.*
		Patrick Drummond.
		Joseph Patten.
		James Howard.
		John Stinson.
1761.	Oct. 16.	Samuel Dennie.*
		William Lithgow.*
		Aaron Hinckley.*
		John North.*
		William Cushing.*
		Jonathan Bowman.
		Patrick Drummond.
		Joseph Patten.
		James Howard.
		John Stinson.
1763.	Feb. 24.	Jedediah Preble.
	Mch. 3.	Jedediah Preble.*
1763.	Sept. 7.	John Kingsbury.
	Nov. 2.	Thomas Goldthwait.*
1764.	Jan. 4.	Thomas Rice.*
		Jonathan Bowman.*
	May 2.	William Crawford.
1766.	Jan. 1.	David Fales.
	Dec. 10.	Alexander Nichols.
1768.	Apr. 20.	Abraham Preble.
1769.	May 3.	Francis Shaw.
		Nathan Jones.
1770.	May 9.	Dudley Carleton.
		Jonathan Longfellow.
1771.	June 12.	Jonathan Bagley.
		James McCobb.
		Arthur Noble.
	Sept. 12.	Stephen Jones.
1772.	June 17.	Nathaniel Thwing.
	Nov. 25.	Ezekiel Pattie.
1773.	Jan. 7.	Obed Hussey.*
	Mch. 6.	Samuel Jordan.
1774.	Feb. 3.	William Gardiner.

CUMBERLAND.

1760.	Oct. 31.	John Minot.*
		Jonas Mason.*
		Ezekiel Cushing.*
		Enoch Freeman.*
		Samuel Waldo.*
		Stephen Longfellow.
		Jacob Royall.
	Nov. 13.	William Simonton.
1761.	Oct. 16.	John Minot.*
		Ezekiel Cushing.*
		Enoch Freeman.
1761.	Oct. 16.	Edward Milliken.*
		Samuel Waldo.*
		Jonas Mason.*
		Stephen Longfellow.*
		Alexander Ross.*
		William Simonton.
	Nov. 20.	Jeremiah Powell.
		William Woodside.
1761.	Jan. 4.	Francis Waldo.
	Mch. 7.	Solomon Lombard.*
		David Mitchell.

Justices of the Peace—Concluded.

1764.	Mch. 7.	William Silvester.	1771.	June 12.	Jonathan Bagley.
		William Thompson.	1772.	June 17.	Richard King.
1767.	May 6.	Daniel Epes.		July 14.	David Wyer, Jr.
1768.	Feb. 21.	Moses Pierson.*		Nov. 25.	William Gorham.
		Theophilus Bradbury.	1773.	Jan. 7.	William Allen.
1770.	May 9.	Thomas Smith, Jr.			

BERKSHIRE.

1761.	June 24.	Joseph Dwight.*	1766.	June 18.	Mark Hopkins.
		William Williams.*	1767.	July 1.	David Ingersoll, Jr.
		John Ashley.*	1770.	May 9.	Samuel Todd
		Timothy Woodbridge.*			Woodbridge Little.
		Perez Marsh.			Joseph Bennett.
1764.	Feb. 1.	John Chadwick.	1771.	June 27.	John Ashley, Jr.
		Daniel Brown.			Nehemiah Bull.
1765.	June 20.	Jonathan Hubbard.			Jahleel Woodbridge.
	Sept. 6.	Elijah Dwight.		July 2.	Elijah Dwight.*
		Israel Stoddard.	1774.	Feb. 10.	Samuel Brown, Jr.

CORONERS.

SUFFOLK.

1692.	May 27.	Capt. Edward Willys.
1699.	Sept. 7.	Joseph Prout.
1700.	June 4.	John Hubbard.
		John Fisher, Jr.
		Samuel Thaxter.
1701.	June 12.	Capt. Ephraim Savage.
1702.	June 30.	Ephraim Savage.
		Samuel Thaxter.
		John Fisher.
1715.	Dec. 9.	Samuel Thaxter.
		Ephraim Savage.
		Josiah Fisher.
1718.	June 27.	Samuel Tyley, Jr.
		John Holman.
		Capt. John Norton.
1718–9.	Feb. 26.	Jonathan Pollard.
1720.	Dec. 19.	Seth Dwight.
1721.	Sept. 9.	Samuel Thaxter.
1728.	June 18.	Nathaniel Rawson.
	Dec. 19.	John Chandler, Jr.
		Seth Dwight.
		Samuel Thaxter, Jr.
		Arthur Savage.
		James Blake.
		Jonathan Sewall.
1729.	Oct. 10.	John Holman.
		Nathaniel Rawson.
	Dec. 20.	Maj. John Chandler.
1731.	Dec. 23.	John Dorrell.
		John Walley.
1731–2.	Mch. 21.	Samuel Swift.
1732.	July 6.	Benjamin Lincoln.
		James Blake.
1733.	May 4.	William Young.
		Richard Gookin.
1734.	Dec. 27.	William Winter.
		John Moorey.
1735.	Apr. 19.	Thomas Andrews.
1736.	June 22.	Henry Adams,
		John Metcalf, Jr.
	Dec. 29.	Edward Lutwyche.
1737.	June 30.	William Royall.
		Jonathan Whitney.

1740–1.	Jan. 2.	Joseph Leasonby.
	— 7.	James Davenport.
1711.	Aug. 4.	John Adams.
1741–2.	Jan. 15.	Elisha Adams.
1743.	Nov. 25.	Nathaniel Gill.
1743–4.	Mch. 6.	James Blake.
		John Walley.
		John Metcalf.
		James Jervis.
		Henry Adams.
		Edward Ruggles.
		John Whitney.
		Joseph Leasonby.
		James Davenport.
		Joseph Miller.
		Nathaniel Gardner.
		Samuel Watts, Jr.
	— 8.	Thomas Gill.
1744.	Sept. 6.	Isaac Bullard.
1745–6.	Jan. 24.	John Thomas.
1747.	Dec. 12.	Seth Brewster.
1749.	Apr. 18.	Thomas Cross.
	— 21.	Ebenezer Mann.
1752.	Feb. 7.	Increase Sumner.
1753.	Jan. 2.	Stephen Kent.
		Joseph Andrews.
	— 4.	Joseph Dean, Jr.,
1755.	June 26.	William Badcock.
	Oct. 10.	David Capen.
1756.	Sept. 14.	Jonathan Collier.
1758.	Apr. 1.	John Harris.
	May 12.	Robert Pierpont.
1759.	Dec. 19.	Thomas Dawes.
		John Morey, Jr.
1761.	Nov. 5.	Nathaniel Gardner.
		Thomas Crafts.
		Robert Pierpont.
		Stephen Kent.
		Increase Sumner.
		Samuel Williams.
		William Badcock.
		David Capen.
		Ebenezer Mann.

Coroners—Continued.

1761.	Nov. 5.	John Thomas.
		Joseph Andrews.
		Elisha Adams.
		John Morey.
		John Adams.
		John Metcalf.
		Joseph Dean.
		Jonathan Collier.
		John Harris.
		Thomas Dawes.
		Ebenezer Pope.
		Andrew Adams.
1762.	Jan. 28.	Thomas Andrews.
		Ezekiel Richardson, Jr.
		Samuel Lethbridge.
	Feb. 4.	Josiah Capen.
	Mch. 4.	Joseph Andrews.
	—— 11.	Abner Ellis.
		Robert Hinsdell.
		Swift Payson.
	Aug. 5.	Asa Richardson.

1763.	Feb. 17.	Jacob Gould.
	July 6.	Samuel Watts, Jr.
		William Oliver.
1764.	May 28.	James Robinson.
	Dec. 5.	Elijah Davis.
1766.	Mch. 12.	James Penniman.[1]
	Dec. 10.	Samuel Holbrook.
1767.	Mch. 25.	Nathaniel Fisher.
1768.	Feb. 24.	John Brewer.
		Joseph Vose.
		Jonathan Ware.
	Apr. 11.	William Crafts.
1769.	July 26.	Thomas Penniman.
1770.	May 9.	Oliver Vose.
	Aug. 30.	George Blackman.
1771.	Apr. 19.	Stephen Whiting.
		Jonathan Dean.
1773.	Aug. 11.	Thomas Browne.
1774.	Feb. 10.	Lemuel Davenport.
	Mch. 4.	Caleb Hayward.

ESSEX.

1692.	July 8.	Timothy Lindall.
		Tristram Coffin.
1697.	Sept. 7.	Daniel Epps.
1700.	June 7.	Maj. Francis Wainwright.
1702.	June 30.	Tristram Coffin.
		Daniel Epps.
		Francis Wainwright.
	Oct. 23.	Capt. John Browne.
1704.	June 15.	Francis Wainwright.
1707.	Apr. 15.	Benjamin Pierce.
1711.	Oct. 26.	Maj. Henry Somerby.
1713.	June 5.	Nehemiah Jewett.
1714.	June 15.	John Newman.
1715.	Dec. 9.	Daniel Epps.
		Nehemiah Jewett.
		Henry Somerby.
		John Newman.
		Richard Travell.
1718.	Apr. 16.	Capt. Peter Osgood.
	June 27.	Daniel Appleton.
	Nov. 20.	Capt. Edmund Greenleaf.
1720.	Dec. 19.	Joseph Allen.
1727.	Dec. 26.	Richard Dummer.
1729.	Aug. 28.	Capt. David Parker.

1729.	Oct. 10.	Peter Osgood.
		Joseph Allen.
		Richard Dummer.
	Dec. 5.	Capt. Thomas Wade.
1733.	June 22.	David Parker.
		Peter Osgood.
		Joseph Allen.
		Richard Dummer.
		Thomas Wade.
1735.	June 27.	Jonathan Stephens.
1735-6.	Jan. 2.	Ebenezer Choat.
		Capt. Joshua Hicks.
	—— 16.	Joseph Allen, Jr.
		Francis Bowden.[2]
1737.	June 30.	Philemon Dane.
	Dec. 29.	Ebenezer Bowditch.
		Joshua Ward.
1737-8.	Mch. 9.	James Pierson.
1738.	July 8.	Enoch Titcomb.
1738-9.	Jan. 12.	Robert Hooper, Jr.
1739.	July 6.	John Lewis.
		Robert Herrick.
1740.	July 5.	Epes Sergeant, Jr.
1743.	Oct. 27.	Benjamin Ives, Jr.

---

[1] Of Medway.   [2] In place of David Parker.

Coroners—Continued.

1743.	Nov.	3.	Henry Rolfe, Jr.	1761.	Nov. 19.	Job Collins.
1746-7.	Jan.	14.	Timothy Hoyt.			Abraham Choate.
1748.	Apr.	15.	William Roby.			Benjamin Goodridge.
1748-9.	Jan.	4.	Daniel Staniford.			John Fisher, Jr.
1751.	June 21.		Henry Herrick.			Samuel Ayres.
1753.	Jan.	4.	Henry Ingals.			John Sawyer.
	Sept.	6.	Benjamin Dutch.			Edward Waldron.
			Daniel Sergeant.			Abel Greenleaf.
	——	11.	Andrew Burleigh.			John Cogswell.
			Robert Harris.	1762.	Feb. 4.	Thomas Choate, Jr.
1755.	Jan.	8.	Francis Corbett.			Daniel Sargent.
	——	11.	Benjamin Woodbridge.			Willis Hall.
			John Chipman.			Thomas Munroe.
			Samuel Lee.			Thomas Gilbert.
	June 26.		Joshua Ward.			James Richardson.
	Oct.	10.	William Bowles.		Mch. 11.	David Pierce.
1756.	July	9.	Samuel Greenleaf.		Apr. 21.	Stephen Choate.
	Sept. 14.		Benjamin Goodridge.			George Newmarsh.
			Daniel Clark.	1763.	Feb. 17.	Edmund Bartlett.
			John Foster, Jr.		July 6.	John Dummer.
			Jonathan Bancroft.	1764.	Feb. 1.	John Dummer.
			David Hale.		Nov. 7.	Jonathan Bradbury.
1758.	Apr.	1.	Greenfield Hooper.	1765.	Jan. 16.	Moses Dole.
1759.	Dec.	19.	Samuel Ayres.	1766.	Nov. 12.	John Orne.
1760.	May	23.	Abraham Choat.	1767.	Mch. 25.	John Stephens.
1761.	Nov.	19.	Ebenezer Bowditch.	1768.	Aug. 3.	Thomas Mason.
			Francis Cabot.	1771.	June 12.	Jeremiah Pearson.
			Andrew Burleigh.		Dec. 10.	Thomas West.
			Henry Herrick.	1772.	June 17.	Daniel Edwards.
			Samuel Goodridge.		Aug. 26.	Moses True, Jr.
			Jonathan Bancroft.	1773.	Jan. 7.	Epes Sergeant, Jr.
			Daniel Clark.		Mch. 2.	John Edwards, Jr.
			Henry Ingall.	1774.	Feb. 7.	Benjamin Massey.
			David Hale.			

MIDDLESEX.

1692.	May 27.	Solomon Phips.	1731.	July 9.	William Wilson.
1694-5.	Mch. 6.	Jacob Green, Jr.,			Moses Boardman.
		Jonathan Prescott.			Abraham Williams.
1702.	June 30.	Jacob Green, Jr.	1732.	July 6.	Joseph Phillips.
		Jonathan Prescott.	1733.	July 17.	Henry Blaisdell.
	Oct. 23.	Andrew Boardman.	1737.	Nov. 10.	Benjamin Gold.
1715.	Dec. 9.	Andrew Boardman.	1738-9.	Jan. 12.	Ebenezer Goddard.
		Jonathan Prescott.	1741.	Apr. 2.	Nathaniel Blodget.
1725.	Sept. 2.	William Wilson.	1742.	July 8.	Thomas Munroe.
1729.	Oct. 10.	William Wilson.	1743.	June 23.	Jonathan Leland.
		Moses Boardman.		Nov. 10.	Phinehas Parker.
		Abraham Williams.	1743-4.	Mch. 6.	Thomas Valentine.

Coroners—Continued.

1743–4.	Mch. 13.	Zechariah Pool.
1744.	Apr. 5.	Thomas Sparhawk.
	Dec. 21.	Benjamin Stone.
1745–6.	Jan. 24.	Josiah Richardson.
1747.	Dec. 12.	Jonathan Fox.
1748–9.	Jan. 4.	John White.
1751.	June 21.	Timothy Brooks.
1753.	Sept. 6.	Jonathan Remington.
1754.	Jan. 25.	Ebenezer Goddard.
		Jonathan Leland.
1755.	Jan. 8.	Joseph Abee.
	—— 11.	Samuel Dakin.
1756.	July 9.	Josiah Whittemore.
	Sept. 14.	Benjamin Easterbrook.
1759.	Mch. 8.	Israel Hubbard.
1761.	Nov. 20.	Israel Hobart.
		Benjamin Easterbrook.
		Josiah Richardson.
		John Remington.
1761.	Nov. 20.	Benjamin Stone.
		John White.
		Josiah Whittemore.
		John Stone.
		Jonas Dix.
1762.	Apr. 21.	Ebenezer Pratt.
		Jonathan Porter.
	July 29.	Aaron Chamberlain.
1763.	Feb. 17.	Joshua Eaton.
		Aaron Chamberlain.
1764.	Mch. 7.	James Fowle, *tertius*.
1766.	Dec. 10.	Jonathan Haywood.
1769.	July 12.	Isaac Farnsworth.
1770.	May 9.	John Abbey.
1771.	June 27.	Josiah Smith.
	Dec. 10.	Abraham Watson.
1772.	Feb. 19.	David Haven.
	Nov. 25.	Samuel Pool.

HAMPSHIRE.

1700.	June 7.	Peletiah Glover.
1702.	June 30.	Peletiah Glover.
		Ebenezer Pomroy.
1715.	Dec. 10.	Peletiah Glover.
		Ebenezer Pomroy.
1722–3.	Jan. 9.	Joseph Hawley.
1729.	Oct. 10.	Joseph Hawley.
1732.	Dec. 28.	William Partridge.
		Peletiah Glover.
1733.	June 22.	Josiah Sheldon.
1731.	Dec. 27.	Chris. Jacob Laughton.
1735.	June 27.	Thomas Ingersol.
		Abraham Burbank.
1735.	June 27.	Ebenezer Pomroy, Jr.
1737.	June 30.	Hezekiah Wright.
1754.	Jan. 25.	William Ingersoll.
		Ebenezer Pomroy, Jr.
1755.	Jan. 8.	Robert Harris.
1756.	Sept. 14.	Phineas Lyman.
1761.	June 24.	Ebenezer Pomroy.
		Robert Harris.
		Phineas Lyman.
1762.	Mch. 25.	Jonathan Leland.
1764.	Feb. 1.	Benjamin Day.
1770.	May 23.	Josiah Rawson.

PLYMOUTH.

1694–5.	Mch. 6.	William Clarke.
1700.	June 7.	Nathaniel Thomas, Jr.
		Joseph Otis.
1702.	June 30.	Nathaniel Thomas, Jr.
		Joseph Otis.
1702–3.	Mch. 18.	David Jacobs.
1715.	Dec. 9.	David Jacobs.
		John Watson.
1719.	Dec. 2.	Thomas Barker.
	—— 9.	Benjamin Warren.
1721–2.	Mch. 16.	Charles Little.
1724.	Dec. 15.	Richard Davenport.
		John Little.
1729.	Oct. 10.	—— Benjamin.
		Richard Davenport.
		John Little.
		David Jacobs.
1731.	Aug. 25.	Benjamin Warren.
		David Jacobs.
		John Sparhawk.

Coroners—Continued.

1733.	June 22.	James Arnold.	1762.	Jan. 28.	Theophilus Cotton.
		Cornelius White.			Nathaniel Foster.
		Samuel Edson.			Seth Bryant.
1733–4.	Feb. 14.	Isaac Lothrop, Jr.,			Daniel White.
	21.	Jacob Jacobs.			Samuel Barker.
1734.	Dec. 27.	Benjamin Tucker.			David Jacobs.
		John Holman, Jr.			Peleg Bryant.
	—— 31.	Nehemiah Cushing.			William Sylvester.
1735.	June 27.	Samuel Barker, Jr.			Nathaniel Sylvester.
1735–6.	Jan. 9.	Ezekiel Turner.			Nehemiah Cushing.
1736.	June 22.	David Clap.			Thomas Turner.
		Joseph Haskell.			James Howard.
	Dec. 29.	John Ruggles.			Benjamin Tucker.
1740.	Dec. 5.	Josiah Sturtevant.			John Haskell.
1743.	Nov. 12.	David Clap, Jr.			Daniel Willis.
1743–4.	Mch. 6.	Nathaniel Clap.			John Clapp, Jr.
1744–5.	Jan. 12.	John Willis.			Amos Turner.
	—— 26.	William Sylvester.			Phinehas Cushing.
	Feb. 9.	Theophilus Cotton.			Increase Clapp.
1746.	Aug. 9.	Samuel Norton.			John Torrey.
1748–9.	Jan. 4.	Peleg Bryant.			Caleb Turner.
	11.	Nathaniel Foster.		Mch. 11.	Joshua Stanford.
1749.	Aug. 18.	Daniel White.		July 29.	Jonathan Cobb.
1753.	Jan. 2.	Nathaniel Sylvester.	1763.	Feb. 17.	John Ruggles, Jr.
1754.	Jan. 25.	Nathaniel Foster.		Dec. 7.	John Wilks.
		Samuel Barker, Jr.	1764.	Nov. 7.	Isaac Little.
	Apr. 19.	Consider Howland.	1765.	Feb. 6.	Josiah Smith.
		Samuel Norton.			Nathan Howard.
		Edward Howland, Jr.	1767.	July 1.	Samuel Savery.
1755.	Jan. 8.	Seth Bryant.	1771.	June 12.	Moses Inglee.
	June 26.	John Clap, Jr.	1772.	June 19.	Hawkes Cushing.
	Oct. 10.	Benjamin Tucker.	1773.	Jan. 19.	Silvanus White.
1756.	Sept. 14.	Thomas Turner.		Mch. 6.	Josiah Edson, Jr.
		Daniel Willis.			

BRISTOL.

1694–5.	Mch. 6.	Nathaniel Payne.	1718.	June 27.	Daniel Carpenter.
1701.	June 12.	Samuel Little.	1724–5.	Feb. 18.	Edward Shove.
		Philip King.	1729.	Oct. 10.	Samuel Royal.
		Thomas Tabor.			Daniel Carpenter.
1702.	June 30.	Samuel Little.			Joseph Mason.
		Stephen Payne.	1732.	July 7.	John Foster,
1711.	Apr. 19.	Charles Church.			John Palmer.
1715.	Dec. 10.	Charles Church.	1733.	June 22.	Samuel Royal.
		Seth Williams.			Comfort Carpenter.
		Constant Church.			John Akin.
1718.	Apr. 16.	William Throop.			Samuel Williams.
	June 27.	Samuel Royall.			Sylvester Richmond, Jr.

Coroners—Continued.

1731.	July 3.	Joseph Russell.	1749.	Apr. 18.	Elnathan Walker.
	Dec. 27.	James Williams.	1754.	Jan. 25.	Ebenezer Dean.
		Elnathan Pope.	1755.	Jan. 8.	John Soule.
		Ephraim Leonard.			John Crane.
1735-6.	Jan. 2.	Zephaniah Leonard.			Joshua Knowles.
	— 9.	Capt. Samuel Cornett.			Timothy Bourne.
1737.	June 30.	Gershom Crane.			Benjamin Williams.
	Dec. 29.	Samuel Williams, Jr.	1756.	Sept. 14.	Isaac Hodges.
1737-8.	Jan. 13.	Josiah Talbot.	1759.	Dec. 19.	Benjamin Day.
		Joseph Hodges.			Daniel Bailey.
1738.	Aug. 12.	Henry Crane.	1761.	Nov. 24.	David Williams.
		Joseph Read.			Daniel Barney.
1740.	Apr. 4.	William Richmond.			John Crane.
	July 5.	David Williams.			Ebenezer Dean.
		William Richmond.			Benjamin Williams.
	Dec. 5.	Ezekiel Carpenter.			John Soule.
1743.	Nov. 3.	Fobes Little.			Isaac Hodges.
1743-4.	Mch. 13.	John Palmer.			Benjamin Day.
		Zephaniah Leonard.			Daniel Bailey.
		Josiah Talbot.			Nathaniel Leonard.
		Joseph Hodges.	1762.	Jan. 28.	Ebenezer Dean, Jr.
		David Williams.			Abiel Perry, Jr.
		Moses Mendall.			Benjamin Williams, Jr.
		Elijah Dean.		Apr. 21.	Caleb Church.
		Joseph Read.			Joshua Richmond.
		Nathaniel Bosworth.	1763.	Feb. 17.	Jonathan Cobb.
		Daniel Barney.			Lemuel Crane.
		Samuel Lee, Jr.			John Ingall.
		Benjamin Wildbore.	1764.	June 8.	John Crane.
1744.	Aug. 18.	John Crane,	1768.	Feb. 24.	Nathan Doggett.
1745-6.	Feb. 8.	Abraham Tucker.	1771.	Apr. 16.	Benajah Barney.
1747-8.	Mch. 1.	Israel Dean.		June 27.	Seth Pope.
1748.	Apr. 15.	Samuel Tyler.	1772.	June 17.	Isaac Greenwood.
	Nov. 8.	Abiel Terry.	1773.	Mch. 2.	William Dean.
	— 18.	Israel Tupper.	1774.	Feb. 7.	James Williams, Jr.

BARNSTABLE.

1694-5.	Mch. 6.	Thomas Freeman.	1715.	Dec. 10.	Ebenezer Hawes,
1700.	June 7.	Shubael Smith.			John Chipman.
		Samuel Freeman.	1717.	Nov. 12.	Samuel Treat.
		Josias Thatcher.	1721-2.	Mch. 16.	Ezra Bourne.
1702.	June 30.	Shubael Smith.			Stephen Skiffe.
		Samuel Freeman.		— 31.	Josiah Knowles.
1702-3.	Mch. 18.	Peter Thatcher.		Sept. 9.	Samuel Annibal.
1710.	June 8.	Ebenezer Hawes.	1727.	Dec. 26.	Ezekiel Cushing.
	Aug. 24.	Seth Williams.	1729.	Aug. 28.	Judah Thatcher.
1715.	Dec. 10.	Peter Thatcher.		Oct. 10.	Nathan Bassett.
		Samuel Freeman.			Ezekiel Cushing.

Coroners—Continued.

1729.	Oct. 10.	Samuel Treat.	1744.	Dec. 21.	Samuel Bourne.
		Josiah Knowles.	1747.	June 27.	Jonathan Bourne.
		Samuel Annibal.	1747-8.	Mch. 1.	Seth Winslow.
		Stephen Skiffe.	1748.	Nov. 18.	Isaac Hinckley, Jr.
1731.	Aug. 25.	Ezekiel Cushing.	1751.	Apr. 25.	David Sears, Jr.
		Samuel Treat.	1753.	Jan. 2.	Barnabas Freemen.
		Samuel Annibal.			Benjamin Gorham.
		Stephen Skiffe.	1755.	Oct. 10.	James Bourne.
		Judah Thatcher.	1758.	June 22.	Heman Stone.
		Thomas Winslow.	1759.	Mch. 8.	Stephen Hallett.
	Sept. 1.	Richard Knowles.	1762.	Jan. 21.	Benjamin Gorham.
		John Knowles.			Samuel Bourne.
		Thomas Clark, Jr.			Joshua Atkins.
		John Davis.			James Bourne.
1733-4.	Feb. 14.	Edward Sturges.			Heman Stone.
		Silas Bourne.			Stephen Hallett.
1737.	Nov. 18.	Samuel Hallett.	1763.	Feb. 17.	Samuel Jenkins, Jr.
1739.	Oct. 5.	Samuel Bourne.	1764.	Feb. 1.	Cornelius Sampson.
1740.	Dec. 5.	William Roach.	1765.	Feb. 6.	Joshua Knowles.
	— 9.	Moses Mendall.			Solomon Freeman.
1743.	Jan. 27.	Joshua Atkins.			Winslow Lewis.
1743-4.	Mch. 6.	Samuel Annibal, Jr.	1768.	Nov. 30.	James Covell.
		John Sturges.			

YORK.

1694-5.	Mch. 6.	Jonathan Hammond.	1746.	Sept. 6.	Henry Simpson, Jr.
1700.	June 7.	Joseph Hammond, Jr.	1747.	Sept. 11.	William Leighton, Jr.
1706.	June 8.	Charles Frost.	1749.	Apr. 18.	John Davis.
1707.	June 5.	Capt. Lewis Bane.		June 29.	Joseph Pope.
1708.	June 15.	Lewis Bane.	1751.	Apr. 25.	Joshua Bangs.
1715.	Dec. 13.	Lewis Bane.	1753.	Sept. 17.	Thomas Scale.
1721-2.	Mch. 9.	Samuel Came.	1754.	Jan. 25.	Elijah Royal.
1729.	June 25.	Joseph Banks.	1756.	July 9.	Benjamin Gerrish.
	Dec. 20.	Samuel Moody.	1758.	June 22.	Jeremy Hill.
		George Hammond.	1761.	Nov. 20.	Elihu Gunnison.
1731.	July 9.	Joseph Banks.			Benjamin Gerrish.
		Samuel Moody.			Henry Simpson.
1733-4.	Feb. 21.	Jeremiah Moulton.	1763.	Feb. 17.	John Frost, Jr.
1734.	June 28.	Elihu Gunnison.			Humphrey Chadbourne.
	Dec. 27.	Jonathan Prebble.			Andrew Bradstreet.
1735-6.	Jan. 2.	Jonas Mason.	1771.	Apr. 16.	Edward Emerson.
1737.	June 30.	Samuel Came, Jr.	1774.	Feb. 7.	Joseph Hobbs.
1740.	June 28.	Daniel Moulton.			Benjamin Staples.

NANTUCKET.

1708.	June 15.	George Gardner.	1751.	June 30.	Daniel Bunker.
1715.	Dec. 13.	Joseph Coffin.	1717.	Sept. 11.	Caleb Bunker.
1720.	Oct. 10.	Peleg Bunker.	1762.	Aug. 5.	Timothy Folger.
		John Butler.			

Coroners—Continued.

DUKES.

1697.	Oct. 14.	John Butler.	1731.	June 30.	Nathan Bassett.
1713.	Dec. 9.	John Butler.			William Hunt.
	—— 13.	Benjamin Hawse.	1732.	July 7.	Simeon Butler.
1716.	June 15.	Nathaniel Bassett	1734.	July 3.	Thomas Daggett.
1717.	Nov. 12.	Nathan Bassett.	1761.	Oct. 16.	Robert Allen.
1721.	Nov. 16.	John Norton.			Thomas Daggett.

WORCESTER.

1731.	June 30.	James Wilder.	1759.	Mch. 8.	Noah Sparhawk.
		Seth Chapin.	1762.	Jan. 21.	John Curtis.
		Joseph Wright.			Josiah Brewer.
1733.	June 22.	Gershom Rice.			Charles Richardson.
1735.	Apr. 19.	Edward Goddard, Jr.			Benjamin Reed.
1737.	June 30.	Othniel Taylour.			Hezekiah Ward.
1737-8.	Jan. 13.	Oliver Wilder.			Josiah Wolcott.
1738-9.	Jan. 12.	Samuel Chandler.			Joseph Hartwell.
1741.	July 16.	William Rawson, Jr.			Manasseh Stone.
1742.	July 8.	Hezekiah Ward.			Edward Raymond.
1744.	Dec. 27.	Joseph Wilder, Jr.			Alpheus Fletcher.
		William Ayres.			Edward Rawson.
1745-6.	Jan. 24.	Gardner Chandler.	——	Mch. 11.	William King.
1746-7.	Jan. 14.	Jabez Lyon.			William Richardson.
1747.	Dec. 12.	Samuel Barton.		Apr. 21.	Nathaniel Green.
		David Wilder.	1766.	Feb. 5.	John Black.
1748-9.	Jan. 4.	John Murray.	1768.	Feb. 24.	Samuel Mower.
		Thomas Hudson.	1770.	May 9.	Mark Lincoln.
1753.	Sept. 17.	Charles Richardson.	1771.	Apr. 19.	Joseph Craig.
1754.	Jan. 25.	Benjamin Reed, Jr.	1772.	Apr. 1.	Nathan Goodale.
		Edward Goddard.		Aug. 26.	Seth Hapgood.
	Apr. 19.	John Caldwell.	1773.	Jan. 19.	Silas Jones.
		Obadiah Rice.			Timothy Ruggles, Jr.
1756.	July 9.	Asa Flagg.	1774.	Feb. 7.	Gardner Chandler.
1759.	Mch. 8.	Nathaniel Adams.			

LINCOLN.

1760.	Oct. 31.	Jonathan Preble.	1770.	May 23.	Mason Wheaton.
1761.	Jan. 24.	Abraham Preble.	1771.	Apr. 19.	Benjamin Shute.
	Oct. 16.	Jonathan Preble.			Daniel McFaden.
1763.	Sept. 7.	Edmund Bridge.	1772.	Mch. 4.	Thomas Boyd.

CUMBERLAND.

1760.	Oct. 31.	Joshua Bangs.	1761.	Oct. 16.	Joshua Bangs.
		Thomas Scales.	1763.	Feb. 24.	Brice McLellan.
1761.	Oct. 16.	Thomas Scales.	1772.	June 17.	Peleg Chandler.

Coroners—Concluded.

BERKSHIRE.

1761.	June 24.	William Ingersoll.	1771.	June 27.	David Sandford.
1765.	June 20.	Israel Dickinson.	1772.	June 19.	Erastus Sergeant.
1771.	June 27.	William Day.	1774.	Feb. 10.	William Goodrich.

NOTARIES PUBLIC.

1692.	July 21.	Sampson Sheaffe, John Higginson.
1696.	June 4.	Stephen Sewall.
1698.	June 3.	John Valentine, to officiate in the absence of Sampson Sheaffe.
1699.	July 25.	Joseph Valentine.
1712.	Oct. 21.	John Valentine and Nathaniel Shannon, for Suffolk.
1715.	Dec. 10.	Nathaniel Payne, for Bristol; Stephen Sewall, for Essex; John Valentine.
1719.	June 27.	Arthur Savage.
	Nov. 25.	Joseph Hiller.
	June —.	Joseph Hiller and Samuel Tyley (Boston): Stephen Sewall (Salem); Stephen Jaques (Newbury); John Dyer (Plymouth); Ebenezer Brenton (Bristol); William Pepperill (Kittery).
1724.	June 12.	Hiller, Tyley, Sewall, Dyer; also Stephen Jaques, Jr. (Newbury); William Throop (Bristol); John Newman, Jr. (Kittery).
1725.	June 15.	Hiller, Tyley, Sewall, Jaques, Dyer; also Timothy Fales (Bristol); Charles Frost (Kittery).
1726.	June 21.	Hiller, Tiley, Jaques, Dyer, Fales, Frost; also Mitchell Sewall (Salem).
1727.	June 28.	Tyley, Sewall, Jaques, Dyer, Fales, Frost; also Benjamin Rolfe (Boston).
1728.	June 12.	Same list, except Nathan Bowen in place of Sewall for Salem.
1731.	Jan. 5.	Tyley, Rolfe, Sewall, Jaques, Fales, Frost; also John Sparhawk (Plymouth).
1732.	July 4.	Tyley, Rolfe, Sewall, Fales, Frost; also Ebenezer Choate (Newbury); Samuel Bartlett (Plymouth).
1733.	June 21.	Same list, adding Richard Dana (Salem and Marblehead).
1734.	June 13.	Tyley, Rolfe, Sewall, Dana, Choat, Fales; also John Winslow (Plymouth); Richard Cutt, Jr. (Kittery).
1735.	June 18.	Same, adding Samuel Sturgis, Jr. (Barnstable).
1736.	June 22.	Tyley, Rolfe, Sewall, Choat, Winslow, Sturgis, Cutt; also Nathan Bowen (Salem); Stephen Payne (Bristol); Moses Pierson (Falmouth).
1737.	July 5.	Same list, adding Joseph Allen, Jr. (Gloucester).
1740.	July 2.	Samuel Tyley, Samuel Gerrish (Boston); Mitchell Sewall, Nathan Bowen, Daniel Witham (Salem); Charles Pierce (Newbury); Edward Winslow (Plymouth); John Sturgis (Barnstable); Stephen Paine (Bristol); Richard Cutt (Kittery); Samuel Moody (Falmouth); Daniel Bunker (Nantucket).
1741.	June 31.	Tyley, Sewall, Bowen, Witham, Pierce, Sturgis, Paine, Bunker; also Ezekiel Goldthwaite (Boston); James Hovey (Plymouth); Jabez Fox (Falmouth).
1747.	June 24.	Ezekiel Goldthwaite and Samuel Holbrook (Boston); Mitchell Sewall, John Chipman, Jr., William Parsons and William Atkins (Salem); Edward Winslow (Plymouth); Solomon Otis (Barnstable); Elihu Gunnison, Jr. (Kittery); Daniel Moulton (York); John Norton (Edgartown); John Bunker (Nantucket).
1749.	June 23.	Same list, with James Jeffry in the room of Sewall (Salem); adding Enoch Freeman (Falmouth).
1750.	June 20.	Goldthwaite Holbrook, Jeffries, Chipman, Atkins, Winslow, Otis, Gunnison, Moulton, Norton and Bunker, adding Daniel Witham (Gloucester) and Stephen Longfellow (Falmouth).

Notaries Public—Concluded.

1751.	June 20.	Same list.
1752.	June 3.	Same list.
1753.	June 19.	Same list, dropping Holbrook and adding Ezekiel Price (Boston).
1754.	Dec. 24.	Same list, adding Charles Chauncey, Jr. (Kittery), in place of Gunnison.
1755.	Dec. 17.	Goldthwait, Price, Atkins, Chipman, Witham, Winslow, Otis, Moulton, Chauncey, Longfellow, Norton and Bunker; adding John Nutting (Newbury), in place of Jeffries.
1756.	June 4.	Same list, adding Thomas Foster, Jr. (Plymouth), in place of Winslow.
1757.	June 8.	Same list, with Edward Winslow (Plymouth), in place of Foster.
1760.	Feb. 1.	Goldthwait, Price, Nutting, Chipman, Atkins, Winslow, Otis, Moulton, Chauncey, Longfellow, Norton and Bunker.
1761.	Jan. 8.	Same list, adding Daniel Witham (Gloucester), and Obed Hussey (Nantucket), in place of Bunker.
1762.	Feb. 4.	Same list, adding also Thomas Gilbert and Elisha Tobey (Bristol); John Wheelwright (Wells); and Thomas Moulton (Lincoln).
1763.	Jan. 27.	Goldthwait, Price, Nutting, Chipman, Witham, Atkins, Winslow, Otis, Gilbert, Tobey, D. Moulton, Chauncey, Longfellow, Norton, T. Moulton, Hussey.
1764.	Jan. 18.	Same list, adding Henry Alline, Jr. (Boston), in place of Price.
1765.	Jan. 13.	Same list, adding Samuel Sawyer (Ipswich); Thomas Smith (Falmouth); John Wheelwright (Wells).
1766.	Feb. 11.	Goldthwait, Alline, Nutting, Sawyer, Chipman, Atkins, Witham, Winslow, Otis, Smith, Gilbert, Tobey, Norton, Hussey, D. Moulton, Chauncey, Wheelwright, Longfellow, T. Moulton.
1767.	Feb. 12.	Same list, adding John Pease, Jr. (Edgartown).
1768.	Feb. 11.	Same list, adding also Nathaniel Gorham (Charlestown).
1770.	Mch. 30.	*Dudson Kilcup* (Boston); Alline, Nutting, Sawyer, *Thomas King* (Marblehead); Atkins, Witham, Gorham, *Ephraim Spooner* (Plymouth); Otis, *Joseph Parker* (Falmouth); *Jerathmeel Bowers* (Bristol); Tobey, Pease, *Stephen Hussey* (Nantucket); D. Moulton, Chauncey, Wheelwright, *Jonathan Webb* (Falmouth); T. Moulton.
1771.	April 11.	Same list; Thomas Bragdon (York), in place of Daniel Moulton.
1772.	April 17.	Same list, with D. Moulton (York), for Bragdon, and adding Winslow Lewis (Falmouth).
1773.	Jan. 28.	Kilcup, Alline, Nutting, Sawyer, King, Atkins, Witham, Gorham, Otis, Parker, Lewis, *Joseph Doane* (Chatham); Bowers, Tobey, Pease, Hussey, D. Moulton, Chauncey, Wheelwright, Webb, T. Moulton.
1774.	Feb. 3.	Same list, adding Ephraim Spooner (Plymouth), and Theophilus Parsons (Falmouth), in place of Webb.

INDEX NO. I.

[Containing all the names in the preceding pages, excepting those of Justices of the Peace and of Coroners which are separably indexed.]

22

INDEX No. II.